The Fire Within The Cult

By
Courtnie J Christensen and
Angela E. Powell

Dedication

I would like to dedicate this book to God, without Him I am nothing, but with Him anything is possible.

And to my mother and two beautiful sisters. Not only did we go through these events together, but we lived to share it with the world. We all make decisions but it's how we grow and learn from them that can help not only ourselves but also others to overcome. I pray that your heart be open to accepting God's love like I have. I pray God heals you, blesses you, and protects you during the next steps on this crazy journey called life. I love you muches ~ Courtnie

Acknowledgements

Courtnie: I would like to thank God who led me through this journey. God let all the glory be Yours. Let this book be edifying to Him who redeemed me, called me by name, and called me His. He has saved me according to His great mercy (Isaiah 43:1). He has healed me and continues to help me grow (1 Peter 1:3-5). I love you Jesus!

I also want to thank Angela E. Powell. She has, and will continue to be an inspiration to me. Getting to know her during the writing of our book has been a blessing. She not only helped me write this book about my past, but she has been an amazing support as I've had to relive the memories of the events that took place. She is truly a God-send and a fantastic author.

Special thanks to Dave and Stephanie Springer for taking me into their home and loving me for who I was, even when things got tough. Stephanie, also, for leading me to the Lord and helping me through Biblical Counseling. You truly are gifted in your calling.

To all my family and friends who have supported me and the writing of this book, thank you! I love you!

Angela: I would like to thank God for creating me with the desire and the gift to write. Thank you for all the learning opportunities, writing and general life events, that brought me to a place where I was able to help bring this book about.

Special thanks to my husband, Craig, for listening to me talk about the progress of this book for three years. For putting up with me while I was so engrossed in the process at times, and for giving up many evenings and weekends with me so I could meet with Courtnie. Thanks to my mom who has also listened to me talk about the process of writing this book for three years. You are my greatest encourager.

From both of us: To our editor, Doreen Marten, thank you for taking your time and doing such a fantastic job helping us get this book polished. To our graphic designer, Aaron De La Rosa. Thank you for being patient with us as we made decisions about the cover, and the eye logo, and then changed our minds. Thank you for working with us. To Alisha Prince, graphic designer and friend, Thank you for all your great ideas and time. And finally, thank you to our readers. You are not alone! God is the creator and there is nothing He can't do. He loves you and is waiting for you. Keep pushing through.

Preface

As co-author of this book and stepmother to an adopted special-needs child, I have witnessed the gut-wrenching effects childhood trauma can have on a person. I've spent much of the past seven years learning how to walk beside people who have experienced traumatic events, to help them find a path out of the emotional ravines where they have been trapped.

I've walked alongside Courtnie, known in this book as Sophia, on her healing journey for three and a half years. To watch someone pour through each difficult memory and each complex emotion, determined to find the root cause of her lifelong struggles and receive healing, is inspiring. It's been an honor to be a member of her trusted circle, to see the pain replaced with joy and restoration.

All of the events in this book are true to Courtnie's memory, but they are the memories of a nine-year-old girl and may not be entirely accurate. The emotions she experienced, and the thoughts she had about what was happening to her and those she loved, are true to her experience of them. Others involved in these events may remember things differently. In some cases, we felt it necessary to change the names of people, locations, and even small details of events to protect certain individuals.

I have seen the anger boil over as Courtnie relived the injustices done to her and her siblings. I've watched the tears spill over as she grieved the damage done to past and, in some cases, present relationships because of the things she endured. But I have also seen her persevere though the pain, seek the advice of God, her biblical counselor, and trusted friends, and I've seen her come out on the other end of this journey with far more peace and joy.

As I've journeyed alongside her to put this story into words, I've watched her relationship with God and with other people change and grow. Writing this book has not been an easy process for either of us, but then, the process of healing from trauma isn't easy, either. The closer we got to finishing this book, the more I saw this story becoming for Courtnie just that—a story, a part of her life that Courtnie has been able to accept as part of her history, but a story that no longer has power over her life or her emotions. It's been a beautiful thing to witness, and I know you'll be encouraged as you read about *The Fire Within the Cult*.

Angela E. Powell

Prologue

"Excellent. If you see someone you don't recognize, I want you to shoot them," said Kevin, handing the now loaded rifle back to me. "Just aim through the scope and pull the trigger."

"You can't be serious." Mom grabbed the firearm from my hand.

"Unfortunately, Grace, I am."

"But she's only ten!"

"Edgar told us they trained her to handle guns at the militia house you stayed in. So well, in fact, she is a better shot than most of us. We don't want to kill anyone, but we've experienced enough thieves and government agents on our land that we've developed a shoot-now, ask-questions-later approach. The more people we have armed, the better," Kevin said.

Mom pointed the rifle toward the front gate of the compound and glanced through the scope. "Oh, you mean like the FBI, who are rolling up with their tanks right now?"

We all looked in the direction she pointed. Several armored vehicles, with the letters FBI on the sides, were making their way along the fence line before coming to a stop. I turned to Mom and noted that she was holding the gun sideways, with her finger curled around the trigger of a loaded weapon pointed at the FBI.

And I'm the one who's not allowed to use a gun.

"Yes, exactly like that. Quickly, follow me to the house," Kevin said.

As we made our way inside, people started running toward us from all directions. They must have had some way to communicate quickly, because in a few minutes everyone living in Freedom Township was in the big meeting room.

"All right, guys and gals, listen up," shouted Kevin over the noise. "This is the day we've planned for; no one is allowed to leave the ranch right now, as it poses a risk and could jeopardize this whole operation. It's time to protect our land. So for your safety and ours, please don't set foot off the property.

"As for food and water, we have enough to feed an army for several years. The ten silos are full of wheat and corn, and the springs give us plenty to drink. Plus, we have a few skilled hunters in our ranks.

"Right now, those parasites need to see the children. They know we won't go down without a fight, and they have a lot more firepower than we do, with those armored vehicles. The FBI won't put the kids in harm's way, which means they'll keep their distance and not force their way in."

"Mommy, what are they talking about?" whispered Eva.

I knew what they were talking about. It was the bus all over again. They were going to make me, Eva, and Melissa walk out there so the FBI could see us.

Chapter 1

18 Years Later

I climbed out of my car, closed the door, and paused, staring up at the large, tan brick building before me. The words *Liberty Church* stood out in bold, white letters over the front entrance.

This is crazy. They can't help me. A pastor? Offering biblical counseling services? Why couldn't I go to a therapist, like a normal person? I forced my feet forward but hesitated again. *What am I doing here?* It wasn't too late to turn back and give up on this idea. But I pulled the door open and found myself in a small foyer. A doorway to my right revealed a sanctuary with red carpet and rows of gray chairs. A lit-up, wooden cross was centered on the far wall above the stage.

To my left was a door that led to what looked like a kitchen and dining area. A small table stood by the doorway with stacks of fliers and brochures covering it, no doubt telling of all the programs and events they offered. In front of me was a staircase leading down to a basement and to my right was the hall Stacy had told me to walk down to reach her office. I headed down the hallway and through the door at the end of it. The walls of the room were painted a pearl white. On the wall to my right hung a whiteboard with dates and events listed, and in the corner near it sat a purple chair. On the left was a white door, closed. In the center of the room was a desk. A middle-aged woman with long, black hair speckled with gray rose and stepped out from behind it. She greeted me with an outstretched hand. "Hi there, I'm Jane. Are you Sophia?"

"Yes," I answered cautiously, shaking her hand. "I'm here to see Stacy."

"She'll be right out. Have a seat and I'll tell her you're here." I walked over to the big purple chair and sat down. *I'll wait one minute, then I'm gone.*

Before the thought had completely passed through my head, a tall woman, probably in her mid-fifties, with shoulder-length blonde hair, stepped into the room. "Hi, Sophia. I'm Stacy. I'm so glad we're finally meeting in person. Please, follow me."

I stood and followed her to a small office at the back of the building. There were no windows in the room, but warm light radiated from a table lamp as well as the single fixture on the ceiling, which made the room feel inviting. Pictures of what I assumed must be Stacy's family lined the walls, and a brown love seat filled a third of the space. I took a seat on the couch, and placed one of the pillows on my lap to lean on.

"Do you want something to drink, water or coffee?" asked Stacy as she sat in a chair across from me. Her manner suggested we were old friends having coffee. This wasn't like a meeting with any religious leader I knew. Weird.

"No, I'm okay."

"How are you doing today?"

I fidgeted with the zipper on my sweatshirt. "Um, great, thanks."

Stacy crossed her legs and leaned forward, resting her arms on her knee. "So, we've talked on the phone a little, but I don't think I ever asked how you found us."

I took a deep breath. "This will sound crazy, but I was on my lunch break at work. I was sitting in my car playing games on my phone and listening to the radio, like I usually do. This voice I've heard in my head for months told me to find a church. I tried to ignore it by turning up the radio, but it got louder and more pronounced. It just kept repeating, 'find a church.' Finally, out of irritation, I yelled 'Fine!' and started to search for churches online. I was angry about it. When I came across Liberty Church, I swear the voice told me to stop, so I dialed the number listed. I apologize for the blunt, rude voicemail I left," I finished in a rush, hoping but not expecting that she would believe me.

"How could I forget that? When I heard it I knew right away I had to call you back," Stacy said, with a hint of a grin. "Let's see, what did you say again? Oh yeah: 'I don't know if you can answer my questions or if you can help me, but if you can give me a call back, my number is ...'" Stacy laughed at the memory. "Why did you wait so long to search for a church?"

I studied her face for a moment before answering. The smile wasn't mocking or fake, and her curiosity seemed genuine, not judgmental. I relaxed a little. "I didn't want to listen because churches have hurt me before with rules and severe disciplinary actions, trying to convince us it's what God wanted. It left me with a lot of pain and questions. I think, because of this, I have a hard time trusting any religious person to tell me the truth."

I winced at the accusatory words, but I couldn't help it. I wanted her to assure me I was wrong, or this would never work.

Stacy didn't seem offended. "Oh, man, if I am religious, Lord help me. I am a follower of Christ. *Religion* excludes people. But yes, I got that impression when we talked on the phone for two hours the other day. I knew you needed to trust me before you'd want to meet with me."

"To be honest, Stacy, when I spoke to your husband, Andy, and left you that voicemail, I didn't expect you to call me back, or even want you to. I just wanted the voice to go away. In fact, I was pretty irritated when your number appeared on my phone, because that meant the voice in my head was real and not my imagination."

Stacy laughed. "Well, I don't think you're crazy, so let's see if I can put your mind at ease and answer your questions."

"I think I'm gay."

I sat back, shocked I had blurted that out to a pastor. It was a true statement, and something I'd been struggling with for some time, so I decided to keep going and throw it all out there. *This could be a short meeting if she treats me like all the other religious leaders I've talked to. If she kicks me out, she kicks me out.*

9

Stacy stopped me before I could continue. "Why do you think you are gay?"

"I don't know. But it doesn't feel right in my guts, and I want it to go away." What was happening to me? I had never admitted that to anyone. "I've been living with two friends, who are also gay, and who are like family to me. I don't see them struggling with it like I have been."

"I think it has something to do with my childhood," I went on. "Almost my whole life I've felt like I've been searching for something. I don't know how to explain it, but whatever this voice is, it wanted me to come here and talk to you and would not give up until I did.

"The trouble is, I've been to churches that reject gay people. How does this church respond? Do you judge them like everyone else?" My heart was thumping. I felt like I was sounding crazy right now.

Stacy laughed. "I love your blunt questions. Sometimes we struggle with what the scriptures seem to be saying. Would you mind if I shared something from the Bible with you?"

I hesitated for a moment and decided I was curious. "Sure."

"Thank you. This is from back in the beginning, in Genesis 1:27. It says 'God created mankind in His own image and He created them male and female.' Do you see? God created Adam and Eve, not Adam and Steve."

"Huh, yeah, I've heard that one," I said, uneasily.

"Unfortunately, there are churches that put rules, laws, and traditions before a relationship with Jesus. That's why it's important to remember the whole Bible. Jesus said, in John 15:12, the most important rule, or commandment, is to love one another like He loves us. This means we as the church, or as Christians, are to love others as He loves us. We are not the judge. He is. Here at Liberty Church, we're not perfect at loving others, but we try," Stacy said.

I sat there for a moment, processing what this meant.

Stacy broke the silence. "If you decide you'd like to continue with counseling sessions once you've told me your story, we can discuss this in more depth at that time. Would you like to share your story? What happened to bring you here today?" She held up her hand, as if cautioning me, "That is, if you're comfortable." She waited patiently for me to decide.

"Okay … I can do that." I took a deep breath and began.

"When I was nine years old, my mom married a man involved in a religious cult …"

10 Months Before The FBI Standoff

"Sophia, wake up! Get. Up. Now!" Mom's voice pierced through the blankness of sleep, and I sat up, wide-eyed, feeling disoriented. I stared at her through bleary eyes as she rushed from my closet to my dresser, grabbing clothes and tossing them on my bed. Her long, naturally curly, dark brown hair bounced as she worked. She was wearing light jeans and a black T-shirt. *It's still dark. Why isn't she in her pajamas?*

Mom snapped her fingers in my face, her green eyes seemed to glow in the bright light of my room.

"Hello, Sophia, can you hear me? Your sisters are in the living room. Get moving!" She gathered up the bundle of clothes and carried them out of the room.

I kicked off the covers with heavy, clumsy feet, pulling Wooby, my favorite blanket, close to me.

"SOPHIA!"

The aggravation in Mom's voice escalated, and I bolted to the front room.

Sapphira, who was fourteen and five years older than me, and my six-year-old sister, Eva, were already huddled on the sofa. Eva had wrapped herself in a comforter, so I could only see her from the nose up. Static-tangled strands of blonde hair stuck out from the sides. Her green eyes were wide and watery, and tears stained her cheeks.

We watched Mom move around the room, tossing clothes into various suitcases laid open on the floor. Sapphira's hazel eyes were wide with worry, but not fear. She played with the ends of her long, dark brown hair, a match for Mom's, which she'd pulled into a braid before bed.

The clock in the hall chimed three times. Why were we up so early?

"Girls, I want you to pack a few toys for a trip," she said, tossing backpacks at us. "And be quick."

"What about Midnight?" asked Sapphira, picking up our black poodle.

"The dog stays. Your aunts and uncles will take care of him," Mom said decisively.

"Where are we going? When will we be back? Why can't we wait until morning?" The questions poured out of my mouth.

"Enough!" Mom pointed toward the hall. "Go."

Her expression told me it was pointless to argue, so I headed to my room. Edgar had to be behind this.

I clutched Wooby and sat on the floor, thoughts whirling. Six months ago, when Mom divorced my stepdad, Isaac, everything had changed, and not in a good way. This guy, Edgar, started coming over almost every day. He was tall, with thick, black hair, and always wore a cowboy hat, jeans, and a tucked-in button-up shirt. At first, he seemed like a fun guy and spent time getting to know me and my sisters. One time, he put me on his shoulders and I farted on him and pretended it was an accident because he was bouncing around.

After a while he started bringing over his weird friends, who didn't say much to us kids. For the most part, they ignored us, and we had to either stay outside or in our rooms while they talked for hours in low voices in the kitchen. They always seemed nervous, always looking over their shoulders, under cars, and into the trees. They all had long beards and dressed like cowboys.

A month after Edgar entered our lives, Mom married him in something called a common-law wedding, and Mom changed her name from Violet to Grace. But Edgar didn't live with us.

Maybe that's why we have to leave in the middle of the night?

At the wedding, we had to wear the ugliest dresses. They had a flower print all over and the shoulders were all puffed up. Afterwards, Edgar told us we couldn't discuss anything with Mom's family, because they wouldn't understand.

I overheard aunts and uncles saying Edgar and his friends worried them. Uncle Bill even pulled me aside and said to call him if Edgar ever did anything to make me uncomfortable.

Yeah, this had to be Edgar's doing. He wasn't here, though, so there was no reason to call Uncle Bill. *Edgar*. Even his name creeped me out.

Mom stormed into the room.

"Sophia, you're slower than molasses. Move." She gathered my pillow and blankets. "Why are you still sitting there? Go!"

Her face turned bright red, reminding me of that time Isaac drank Tabasco straight from the bottle and I could have sworn steam came out of his ears. I started to laugh, but stopped myself and looked at Mom. She hadn't noticed.

If I refused to go, would she leave me here? I decided being left alone scared me more than Edgar did, and I scrambled to my feet to change clothes. Grabbing the backpack Mom gave me, I stuffed some toys and books in it and ran outside. The chilly night air made me shiver. I glanced at Mom after putting my bag in the car and, when she wasn't looking, ran back inside to grab my jacket from the coat closet by the door.

When I returned, Sapphira was in the front seat and Eva the back, holding her favorite doll. I realized that if I hurried, I could get my favorite toys, too. I rushed to the playground set, grabbed my dump truck and excavator from under the slide, and then ran to the car. It was a red Buick Skylark. According to my cousin and Sapphira, whom I had overheard talking a few weeks back, it could go really fast. I had never been in it when it was going really fast, but the thought came to me that since Mom was acting like we were running away, maybe I would get to experience it.

Mom stood next to the car, waiting for me. I tossed the toys into the trunk, and she closed it. "Get in and buckle up," she said.

I hesitated at the sound of Midnight barking from inside. "Can we please bring the dog?"

"No, Sophia. In the car," she snapped.

I climbed in and cringed as Mom slammed my door shut.

"Where are we going?" Sapphira asked.

"To meet Edgar."

I knew it! "In the middle of the night?" I asked.

"Quiet, I need to think," Mom said as we backed out of the driveway.

I hugged Wooby, leaving a corner of the blanket on the window's edge so I could rest my head there without too much discomfort.

After driving for what seemed like forever, we pulled into the parking lot of a castle, or at least that's what it looked like to me. Lights embedded in the building and on the lawn lit up the walls. A tall, black iron fence surrounded the property. I shook Eva to show her, but she was fast asleep.

"Are we going to live here?" I asked.

"No, hush. Try to sleep, we'll be on the road all night," Mom said.

"Sophia, will you switch me seats?" asked Sapphira.

I nodded and climbed over the seat, being careful not to elbow or kick Mom, as Sapphira got out of the car and walked around to the backseat. The front window gave me a better view of our surroundings. Empty flower beds lined the sidewalks. Leaves skipped along the ground, driven by the wind, and small, ornamental trees wrapped in white lights were evenly spaced throughout the parking lot.

I'd seen photographs of large buildings similar to this one hanging in the Mormon Church ward we attended occasionally, but never in person. People at the church called it a temple.

Mom clutched the steering wheel and stared at nothing, while her lips moved as if she was talking to herself, or praying. In the backseat Eva snored quietly. Sapphira had her eyes closed, but I didn't think she was asleep yet. I refused to let myself sleep. No, I would be ready and waiting when Edgar arrived.

I hugged Wooby to my chest and sat as straight as possible, away from the tempting comfort of the window. I needed answers. Fat snowflakes drifted around us and slowly covered the windshield. Mom turned on the wipers before the snow totally blocked our view of the outside.

Ten minutes passed. It felt like an eternity. Waiting was a boring job, and I slumped in my seat.

Mom patted my leg. "Put your seat belt on, Sophia. We're leaving."

"Where are we going?" I asked, sitting up a little straighter.

"We're going to meet Edgar."

I slumped in the seat again as the car moved. The wipers had a hypnotizing effect and my eyes got heavier and heavier.

Chapter 2

The unrelenting wail of sirens pulled me from sleep. As I opened my eyes, I was blinded by bright morning sunlight.

Seeing Edgar in the driver's seat sent shivers jolting up my spine. His uncombed, black hair curled every which way, and his eyes were wide. He wore a wrinkled red and white flannel shirt, and his cowboy hat sat on the dash. He looked like he hadn't groomed himself in several weeks; his beard was longer and looked dirtier than usual. He tapped on the steering wheel and stared out the rearview mirror, his mouth drawn into a tight line.

I was in the center of the front bench seat now. Mom was to my right, snoring, her head resting on the passenger side window. I scooted closer to her. When did he join us? And where was that noise coming from?

I peered out the windows. The snow had disappeared, unfamiliar mountains surrounded us, and we were parked off a road I'd never been on before, in front of a bridge. I twisted around to check on my sisters: Eva still slept, and Sapphira was staring out the rear window at the red and blue lights of a police car.

Sapphira faced forward again just as Eva opened her eyes.

"Where are we?" she yawned.

"Hush. Keep your heads down, don't make eye contact with the officer, don't make a sound," ordered Edgar.

Mom woke with a start and elbowed my shoulder. "Ow," I cried, rubbing the spot.

"Move over and quit crowding me." Mom shoved me toward Edgar. "Why are we stopped?"

"Shut up. Everyone just shut up," said Edgar.

The policeman walked to the driver-side window and knocked. From the corner of my eye I saw the cop look at each of us.

"License and registration."

"What's the trouble?" asked Edgar.

"Are you aware it's illegal to park on the side of the road this close to a bridge?"

"No sir, I am aware that it's illegal to park on a bridge, but I thought I was okay here. My family and I are on vacation and I got tired, so I pulled over to rest."

Edgar dug his wallet out of his back pocket. "Grace, can you get the registration from the glove compartment?"

She did and passed the paper to him. Edgar handed over the requested documents without another word, and the cop strode back to his car.

No one spoke. After several minutes, I glanced at the back seat again. Sapphira still bent her head obediently, but Eva stared wide-eyed at me, both of us forgetting we weren't supposed to look up and too curious to obey.

Edgar tapped on the steering wheel and sighed. "This is taking too long. He shouldn't even need to see documents for this. They have to know something."

Mom and Edgar exchanged looks, and I wondered what they said to each other through that unspoken conversation.

I couldn't see the policeman until he climbed out of his patrol car and headed our direction again.

"Eyes on the floor, girls," Edgar snapped at me and Eva.

Facing forward, I kept my head bent just enough to not get into trouble.

The officer handed the documents to Edgar. "I will let you off with a warning this time. Enjoy your vacation."

"Thank you, sir," Edgar said with a smile, handing Mom the paper and ID, and the cop left.

"Since you're awake, Sophia, climb in back with your sisters," Mom ordered.

As I unbuckled and crawled over the seat, to sit in the middle between my sisters, I heard Mom whisper to Edgar, "See? Everything will be okay."

"Can we eat now?" Eva asked.

"At the next town we'll stop and get food," Edgar said. "Until then, no more complaining."

"How long will that be? I have to pee," whined Eva.

I chuckled. *This guy has no clue what he's in for.*

"We're thirty minutes away from the next town. You can climb out and go here, or hold it," said Edgar.

Eva scrunched her face into a pout. "There aren't any bathrooms here, and people driving by will see me."

"Where are we going?" Sapphira asked in a timid voice.

"That's none of your concern," said Edgar.

Eva wriggled in her seat. "I need to go potty now, Momma."

"Come on, Eva, I'll help you," Mom replied.

They both climbed out of the car and walked over to a bush. Mom helped Eva squat so she wouldn't get her pants wet.

"All aboard," she said moments later, as she strapped Eva into her seat before climbing back into the front. "Let's go."

Thirty minutes later, we stopped at a grocery store. "I don't want to stop a lot, so you'll eat what we get. And don't drink too much, either. I'm not stopping for bathroom breaks every hour," Edgar said.

Sapphira, Eva and I went to the restroom while he and Mom bought a cooler and food supplies. After making sandwiches, we were on the road again, only stopping for rare bathroom breaks and to stretch our legs.

We tried entertaining each other with road trip games such as I Spy, but Edgar wouldn't shut up about what to do if the police stopped us again. My sisters and I slept most of the drive just to avoid listening to him.

As the sun set on the horizon, I became restless and couldn't keep quiet anymore. "Can we stop?"

"No, we'll stop in an hour," Mom said.

I sighed and kicked the seat in frustration.

Edgar reached back and slapped my legs. "Do not disrespect your mother."

I wanted to punch him in the head.

"Edgar!" Mom screamed. In his distraction, he'd let the car drift onto the gravel beside the road. Sapphira's head rolled onto my shoulder as Edgar pulled the wheel to get us back on the pavement. The jerking movement of the car woke both Eva and Sapphira.

"You almost caused us to get into an accident," Edgar scolded, glaring at me in the rearview mirror.

I rolled my eyes at him, knowing he wouldn't see me.

Lights flashed and a siren sounded.

"Great. Here we go again," said Edgar.

"All right, girls, you know the drill. Heads down, no sound," said Mom.

Still angry, I folded my arms and stared straight ahead until Sapphira forced my head downward.

"Don't be an idiot," she whispered.

Sapphira looked scared, so I listened, for her sake.

Edgar rolled down the window as the officer approached.

"License and registration."

"Can I ask why you pulled us over? I wasn't speeding."

The cop didn't answer right away, but shone a flashlight in each of our faces. I clenched my fists. "Your d-driving was erratic b-back there." The officer seemed to have trouble saying some of his words.

"Yeah, sorry about that. The girls were acting out. I guess I got a little distracted." Edgar handed over the papers and the officer disappeared.

"I should go. We're close to the meeting place," Edgar said, watching the rearview mirror intently, his jaw moving back and forth.

"No. The worst you'll get is a ticket," Mom said.

"He's in his car. When he gets out, then I'll go."

"No! It's too dangerous! Besides, think of the others."

Edgar's eyes met mine in the mirror. I smirked and he glared at me.

Silence filled the car until the policeman came back. I wanted to get out of this stupid car, go home and snuggle with my dog and Wooby, and forget any of this had happened.

I jumped when the policeman knocked sharply on the window.

"Everything all right, sir?" asked Edgar.

"The plates on this car match a vehicle reported stolen this morning. Please g-get out with your hands raised."

"I knew it wouldn't be long before my family would try something like this," said Mom. "Please sir, this car is mine—my name, Violet, is on that registration."

He looked over the documents again. "Sorry, I still have to take you in for questioning to investigate these claims. We'll get this taken care of at the station. Sir?" The cop took a couple of steps back from the door, his hand resting on his open gun holster.

Mom looked back at us. "Girls, it will be all right. This is a big misunderstanding and we'll get it all sorted out. You don't need to be afraid."

Edgar smiled, his voice dripping with fake concern. "Yeah, we'll be back on the road, enjoying our vacation soon."

If he was trying to make us feel better, it didn't work; more likely he was trying to fool the cop with this happy family routine.

"Sir, p-please exit the vehicle with your hands raised. Ma'am, you c-can follow us with the children." The officer's stutter seemed to get worse as the tension increased.

"Is that necessary, sir?" asked Mom, clearly frustrated.

"I'm afraid so."

Another officer walked up on Mom's side of the car.

"Are we going to jail?" I asked.

"Mommy, what's happening?" asked Eva.

Edgar opened the door and got out. "It'll be okay, Grace. If anything happens to me, I'll use my one call to have Richard come to meet you."

21

The cop handcuffed Edgar and took him to the police car. Mom exited and spoke with the second officer. As she climbed behind the wheel, a second police car pulled up, in front of ours. We sat in silence for a few minutes. A third patrol car pulled up next to us. On the side of the car, I read *Oklahoma City Police.* Despite our situation, it was a relief to know where we were. With one police car ahead of us and another behind, we headed toward the station.

"Listen, girls. These pigs can't ask you questions if I am not with you, so if they do, you don't answer. Got it?"

"I'll make sure we all stay quiet," said Sapphira.

At the station, an officer took us inside the brown brick building, into a room with a mirror, a metal table, and four plastic chairs.

"I'm Officer Lovell," he said, "and this is Rebecca Summer. Ms. Summer will sit with the children and make sure they're comfortable while we take care of the car situation."

Mom followed the police officer from the room, shooting us a meaningful glance as she walked away.

Ms. Summer wasn't in a police uniform. She was tall and skinny, about Mom's age, with a tanned face and red lipstick; her long, dark hair was pulled into a half ponytail. She wore a black skirt with a blue blouse and a matching black jacket with a badge that hung from the pocket with the letters CPS on it.

"Hi there," she said, smiling, and grabbed the fourth chair, moving it to the far corner before taking a seat and writing something in her notepad, glancing at us every so often.

"I'm hungry," whined Eva.

"Shh, we'll eat when we're on the road again," Sapphira said.

"If we get to leave," I said.

"Sophia, don't talk that way. You'll scare Eva."

"I can have the officer bring snacks in," chimed in Ms. Summer. *She speaks.*

Three pairs of eyes stared at her, but before any of us could respond, Officer Lovell popped his head in the door. "How are we doing in here?"

"The girls would like something to eat," said Ms. Summer.

"I'll see what I can find." He smiled at us and disappeared.

"What if Edgar is a criminal?" I whispered to my sisters, eyeing Ms. Summer.

Eva whimpered and her eyes filled with tears. "They can't take Mom away. Where will we go?"

Sapphira gave me a dirty look.

"Back to Utah … and our dog," I added, hoping to calm my little sister.

Eva folded her knees to her chest and rested her head on them. "Edgar was right. The police are bad."

Sapphira and I exchanged glances but kept quiet. I noticed Ms. Summer raised her eyebrows at Eva's comment and wrote something on the pad of paper.

Officer Lovell returned holding a tray of grapes, cheese, and crackers. Another policeman followed, carrying bottled water and plates.

Eva lifted her head, eyeing the officers warily.

"Help yourselves, girls," said Officer Lovell, placing the tray on the table in front of us.

Eva hesitated for a moment but couldn't resist and stood to fill a plate. Sapphira and I waited for the two police officers to leave the room before grabbing anything for ourselves.

"So, it sounds like your family is taking a road trip. Going anywhere fun?" asked Ms. Summer as we munched.

I glanced at Sapphira, who just stared at her plate, and Eva, who kept stuffing her face. Mom said we shouldn't talk to the police without her there, but this wasn't a police officer.

"Girls, I understand how scary this may all seem. I want you know you're safe here." Ms. Summer's knee bobbed up and down and she kept biting her lip, as though she were nervous.

Again, none of us responded. My teacher at school had told me it was a police officer's job to protect us in emergencies. But this wasn't an emergency. They had brought us to a place for criminals, put us in a scary room, took our mom away and left us with a strange lady. I decided it was best not to say anything and went back to my plate.

She tried again. "The man you're with, is he your father? He's not, is he?"

"No, he isn't," I muttered under my breath.

I glanced at my sisters and they stared back at me. Sapphira looked angry, Eva just confused.

"Are you afraid of Edgar? Does he ever hurt you?"

My anger returned. "Who are you, and why are you so nervous?"

Ms. Summer looked at me, her bottom lip quivered, and she stood and left the room.

I leaned back in my chair and smiled, satisfied I'd gotten rid of the strange woman.

A few minutes later, Officer Lovell walked in and sat in the chair Ms. Summer had vacated. "Girls, we almost have everything taken care of, and your mom will come to get you soon."

"I want to see her now! I want my mom." I stood and ran out the open door. "Mom? Mom, where are you?"

Officer Lovell followed me out. "She's over here, kiddo, I'll show you."

I followed him with my eyes; I didn't want him to force me into another room. He knocked on a door, and when it opened, Mom stepped out.

I ran to her, wrapping my arms around her waist. "Mom!" Tears sprang from my eyes. I was determined not to let her out of my sight again.

"What's going on? What have you been doing with my girls?"

"We gave them snacks and water, and asked how the road trip was going, but the girls were worried about you," said Officer Lovell.

"The lady asked us questions," I said.

"You're questioning my girls without me there? That's illegal, and I demand you let us go right now. There's no reason to hold us here. You know the car is mine."

"Ma'am, I assure you, we only made conversation with the girls," said Officer Lovell.

Why was he lying? Was Edgar right about the police?

Another policeman stepped out of the room Mom just left, shrugged, and shook his head at Officer Lovell, who rubbed his hand over his face several times. "If we've resolved the issue, you're free to go. The keys are at the front desk. But we discovered Edgar has warrants, so he won't be joining you."

Mom grabbed my hand and we collected Eva and Sapphira and headed to the exit. I glanced over my shoulder. Everyone stared after us with sad expressions. *Why are they sad?*

Once we were outside, Mom paced.

"Where's Edgar?" asked Sapphira.

"He has to stay here, but someone is coming to show us the way to the others."

"What others?" I asked.

"Never mind, just be quiet."

"I'm tired of being quiet! All we've done on this trip is be quiet." I stormed off to explore the parking lot.

"Don't wander too far, Sophia," Mom said.

"I won't," I yelled back.

I balanced on the edge of the sidewalk and had Sapphira time me while I ran as fast as I could around the parking lot. A sense of freedom washed over me, and I smiled at the thought of Edgar not coming back. As we played, I felt safe for the first time since we'd left home. I glanced back at Mom to see if she was watching me, but she wasn't.

Our escort arrived. He was a lanky, older guy. His hair was dark, speckled with gray, and wrinkles appeared between his eyes, making him look grumpy even when he smiled. My sense of freedom vanished at the sight of him. He shook Mom's hand and said, "I'm Richard. Please follow me to the next stop." He climbed into his car.

"Girls, it's time to go."

As soon as we were all buckled into our seats, I grabbed Wooby and burrowed my face into it. The few moments of playtime and fresh air had done me good, and my restlessness had vanished. Before long I was asleep, happy to be unconscious for another leg of this horrible road trip.

Chapter 3

It felt like only minutes passed before Mom shook me awake. "Come on, girls, we're switching cars."

I stretched and yawned. Blackness darker than I'd ever experienced surrounded us. "Where are we?"

"We're here to meet up with Edgar's friends. Now, out of the car," snapped Mom.

I obeyed, feeling my way along the side of the car toward a faint red glow in the distance. I could hear crickets chirping and leaves crunching under my feet.

As I reached the front of the car, I stood still a moment, letting my eyes adjust, and then a gruff voice came out of the darkness ahead of me, making goose bumps rise on my arms.

"Follow me," said the voice.

Mom grabbed my hand and pulled me to her. My eyes were starting to adjust, and now I could see the outline of trees towering above us.

We walked toward the glow and found someone sitting beside a campfire, with three tents set up behind him. As we drew closer, I could see that the voice from the darkness belonged to Richard, the man we'd followed from the police station. The other man walked up to Mom and shook her hand.

"Thank you for helping us," she said.

"No problem. I'm Jack. Sam is moving your things from your car to one of our trucks, since yours is compromised. Here are the keys. It's parked next to this blue tent behind me. Richard will lead you to the next camp. When we find out how to free Edgar, we'll join the rest of you."

Jack looked to be in his early twenties, tall and stocky, with dark hair. He looked like a much younger version of Richard. In the dim firelight I could see he didn't have a beard like the others, and behind his black-rimmed glasses, his eyes were a dark color.
Mom took the keys. "Thank you."

Within minutes we were off again.

"What did he mean when he said our car was 'compromised'?" asked Sapphira.

"The cops know our vehicle and might tail us. We'll be driving the rest of the night, so try to sleep."

"What happens when we get to the next campsite?" I asked.

"Do we have to go camping? I hate camping. There are too many bugs," Eva complained.

Mom gave an exasperated sigh. "The less you girls know, the better. Now get some rest."

Pale light filtered through orange and yellow leaves when we stopped again. I hadn't slept but had been told to stay in the truck. My restless movements woke Eva, who looked around for the others, puzzled. "Where's Mom, and Sapphira?"

"Not sure. Mom told me to stay with you until you woke up. Let's go find them."

The air outside was chilly enough to make goose bumps appear on my arms, and it smelled of damp leaves and wood. I heard voices and followed the sound until a group of people standing in front of a neighboring trailer came into view. I spotted Mom and our big sister.

"Girls, we're staying here until Edgar can rejoin us," Mom said, waving us over. She motioned to a yellow trailer. "We will get your things and take them inside after I introduce you to everyone. This is Stewart and Lindsey," she said, indicating the couple standing next to her. "Stewart is the leader here and they have a daughter named Hannah, who will come for a visit later, and this is Becky, Mike, and their son Tim," she finished, nodding toward the remaining members of the group.

Stewart instantly gave me the creeps. When his green eyes met mine, they looked dull and less than amused. He was tall and skinny, wore jeans and a tucked-in, long-sleeved white button-up shirt. He had medium length, dirty-blond hair, with a short beard to match. He stood motionless. What made it worse was that he kept staring at me, Sapphira, and Eva. It made my stomach knot up, and I instantly hated him.

Lindsey also had blond hair, pulled into a ponytail, and wore a long, gray cotton skirt with boots to match, and a white blouse. She was tall and heavy.

I recognized Mike and Becky; they'd been to our house in Utah a few times. Becky was short and a little chubby, with shoulder-length black hair and big, round bangs. She wore a long black skirt and a white blouse, similar to Lindsey's, tucked into it. Her eyes looked a little tired and sad, but her face was friendly.

Mike had short brown hair, neatly combed and trimmed, with a long beard. He wore jeans and a tucked-in, button-up shirt like Stewart's, only blue. The men were all dressed in a style similar to Edgar's customary outfit, except the shirts were a solid color instead of plaid.

We headed back to the truck, which, in the light, was the ugliest truck I'd ever seen. Half of it was green and half red, each half apparently from a different vehicle, with a seam showing where someone had welded the two together. Shaking my head in disgust, I pulled my suitcase from the back. Sapphira came behind me, grabbed her bag and Eva's, handed it to her, and headed toward the yellow mobile home.

The trailer was decent enough, but small. One bedroom contained two bunk beds, so we assumed it was ours and put our suitcases in there before grabbing the rest of our things. I refused to call this place "home," so I would unpack nothing.

"Has Mom told you why we're staying here?" I asked Sapphira, figuring she knew more about our situation, since I'd had to stay in the car.

Sapphira shook her head and continued emptying her suitcase into drawers next to the single bed in our room. "Mom and Edgar are married, and these are Edgar's friends. That's all I know. If you guys are hungry, Mom said the kitchen is full of food and we can help ourselves to it."

Eva ran awkwardly toward the kitchen while I looked around the rest of the trailer.

When I returned to the kitchen, Eva was sitting at the small table, her mouth drawn into a pout.

"What's wrong?" I asked.

"There's no cereal, pancakes, or anything, just gross stuff."

"Gross stuff like what?"

"Wheat bread, rice, canned veggies, stuff like that."

I walked over and checked the fridge and cupboards. Eva was right. They'd shopped for a health nut, not a bunch of kids. "Well, there's bread. Do you want toast?"

"I didn't see butter or jam in there, but I guess so."

"Sapphira?"

"No thanks, I'm okay," she called from the bedroom.

I took out the bread and made toast for myself and Eva. As we ate, a knock sounded on the door.

"I'll get it!" shouted Eva, her mouth full of bread. Crumbs flew everywhere.

"Ew, gross, Eva," I said, chuckling.

"Sorry." Eva ran to the door and opened it. "Oh, hello."

A girl wearing a gray dress with blond hair like Lindsey's, who looked older than me, stood in the doorway. I was seeing a theme here with everyone's clothing, and I didn't like it.

"Hi! I'm Hannah. Can I come in?"

"Sure. I'm Eva." Eva moved aside so Hannah could enter.

"Mom said new kids would join us today. I'm so glad. I've been the only kid for a while now. Well, except for Tim, but he's only four and not much fun to play with."

"This is my sister, Sophia, and my other sister, Sapphira, is in our room putting stuff away," Eva said.

The skinny girl waved at me, and I waved back.

"How old are you?" I asked curiously.

"Eleven."

Hannah's eyes were as dull as Stewart's.

Eva grabbed Hannah's hand. "Will you still play with me, even though I'm only six?"

Hannah laughed. "Of course. It's been a long time since I've had other children to play with."

"Why are all these people living here?" I asked.

"Dad says we're looking for a place to create a new community."

"What does that mean?"

"It's a place we can obey God freely without government interference. And by the time we find the right place, I might be old enough to marry. Mom says she's already seeing signs that I'm blooming."

I hesitated before firing off another question. If I was going to get bizarre answers like that, maybe I should find someone else to ask. I tried a simpler topic. "Do you go to school?"

"I'm homeschooled. You will be, too."

"Who will be my teacher?" asked Eva. "My teacher at home, Ms. Simpson, was super awesome."

Hannah cocked her head to one side. "No one. And you need to forget about Ms. Simpson, because she isn't part of our community. Our parents tell us what to study, then we study for a few hours, and that's it."

That didn't sound promising. How were we supposed to teach ourselves things we didn't know? Something was off about this girl. There was something … empty about her.

"How long have you lived here?" I asked.

"In the trailers? Only a month. Want me to show you the place? I can show you where I live and where the grownups have their meetings."

Eva and I both agreed, glad to be doing something after sitting in the ugly truck for so long.

I told Sapphira we were leaving, and we left to go explore our new surroundings. Six trailers stood in a row, separated by a few feet of grass. A clearing where some logs had been arranged like benches sat opposite the trailers at the bottom of a small hill. From there we could see a small white church in the distance, with a cemetery behind it.

A dirt road lay several yards behind the trailers. I stopped, amazed at the tall, beautiful trees lining both sides of the road and bending inward to create a tunnel of colorful leaves that rained down whenever the wind blew. I had never seen so many trees before. I didn't want to leave the road, but Hannah insisted.

It took only five minutes to see the whole neighborhood … community. Whatever it was, the place was small.

During the tour, Hannah told us the rules of our new home. We had to stay within eyesight of the trailers. The thick trees were our boundary, which meant we weren't able to go far. No disturbing the adults during their meetings, and no attending the meetings. We could see the dirt road from the trailers, but we couldn't go near it without an adult.

As Hannah spoke, I realized the list of things we couldn't do stretched a lot longer than the ones we could.

Hannah mentioned there was a small town near the church where everyone bought groceries. Store trips were apparently the only time Hannah left the community. She showed us how the dirt road curved around, and not too far after the curve was where the town started.

Eva perked up at the mention of a store. "Do they have candy there?"

Hannah gave Eva a funny look. "Probably, but we can't have that."

Eva's face fell. "Why not?"

"Our bodies are holy temples. You shouldn't put garbage into something holy."

Eva looked confused, and I knew what she was thinking: Since when was candy *garbage*?

"What else can't we have?" asked Eva.

Hannah sighed. "Lots of things. You'll find out."

Eva and I exchanged glances.

"Did you know there are lots of black people in town? A lot of them go to that white church over there, so you'll get to see them on Sunday," said Hannah, changing the subject.

"Edgar told us black people are dangerous and we shouldn't talk to them," said Eva.

"That's what my parents say, too. I've never seen them do anything dangerous, but I guess it's better to be safe than sorry."

"There aren't many black people in Utah. If we had stayed there, we would be safer," I said sarcastically.

"My daddy says they're black because God cursed them and their dark skin is a reminder of the punishment they got for disobeying God. He also says they're dangerous because, instead of leaving after the government set them free from slavery, they stayed and tried to make the white people flee the land. They don't believe in God and don't want white people around, either."

"Why do they go to church, then?" I asked.

Hannah shrugged. "My dad says there are lots of false religions out there ..."

For the rest of the morning and afternoon, Eva and I played with Hannah. She showed us her Barbie doll collection, which did not interest me at all, but it made Eva happy. When I showed her my trucks, she took us to a small creek so I could dig in the mud. They both brought dolls and pretended to be on a camping trip.

Since the dolls didn't have a tent to use, I offered to use the trucks to build a fort in the mud so they would have somewhere to live. I found the perfect place a few feet away and sunk the teeth of the excavator into the damp dirt.

Above me, I could hear men talking in angry voices, but I couldn't make out what they were saying very well. I stopped digging and strained my ears.

"He's one of ours, and we will help him. That's that," Richard said.

The other man had his back toward me and his voice didn't carry well. He didn't look like anyone we'd met earlier in the day, but I thought he said something about causing problems. Were they talking about Edgar?

"Are you done yet?" shouted Eva.

Startled, both men stopped talking and looked in our direction. The man I hadn't seen before had a leathery, tanned face and sand-colored hair.

Richard's eyes met mine and he squinted. "You eavesdropping, little girl?"

I shook my head and focused on my task, and when I glanced up again, the men were gone.

Mom called us back to the trailers around dinner time. She had made spaghetti for dinner and gave us strawberry punch. When we finished, I helped Sapphira with the dishes.

"Girls, there are rules here. You must stay in the trailer after dinner. Understood?"

"Why do we have to stay inside, can't we go play?" I whined.

"That's another thing. Hannah's Mom told me you ask far too many questions, Sophia. When you need to know something, they'll tell you."

I rolled my eyes and continued drying the dishes.

"Finish your drink, Sophia. Hannah's Mom brought that over as a special treat. You may not get any more for a while."

"Okay." It was strange that Hannah's parents gave us junk food as a treat when Hannah said she couldn't put junk in her body. Could it be left over from before they started the community? I placed the pan I'd been drying on the counter and chugged the last of the punch in my glass.

"I have to go out for a while. You girls behave, and if I'm not back by eight, get yourselves to bed."

Eva played with her dolls, and Sapphira plopped on the small couch with a book. I stared out the window toward the big fire pit, since there was no TV in the trailer. Questions raced through my mind. What were they doing, and why couldn't we know about it? I considered sneaking out to listen, but when I stood up a wave of tiredness suddenly swept over me. After sleeping through our long drive, it was weird I was so tired, but maybe I had run around more than I thought.

"Guys, I'm going to go to bed," I announced.

"'Night," said Eva.

I shuffled into the bedroom and tried to change into jammies. My arms and legs were heavy, and I had a hard time getting my limbs to go into the correct holes. When I'd managed to get a night shirt on, I gave up on the bottoms and collapsed into bed.

Chapter 4

Hannah is a tattletale. I came to this conclusion after our second day at the trailer park.

"Sophia, Lindsey tells me you walked to the road earlier today. You know that's against the rules," Mom said after she returned from one of her secret meetings.

I had thought Hannah and Eva were busy playing dolls when I left to enjoy the trees behind her house. They certainly didn't notice when I stopped playing with them and investigated the rest of Hannah's house instead.

It might not seem like she's all there, I thought, *but I will have to be more careful around her.*

The adults had three long meetings every day. They met by the fire pit in the morning for two hours. After lunch, they disappeared into the last trailer on the row for a couple of hours, and in the evening they gathered around the firepit again. So I knew they hadn't seen me breaking the rules.

Mostly, we were left to ourselves, but Richard sometimes came to check on us. He carried a large paddle with holes in it and threatened to use it if we misbehaved. I wasn't sure if he was serious, so I tried to be careful with my words and actions around Hannah.

"Sapphira, Stewart wants you to join the meetings from now on, so after lunch you'll come with me," said Mom.

I perked up. I figured if they allowed Sapphira to go, she could tell me what happened.

"Do I have to?" Sapphira asked.

"Yes, you're considered an adult in this community, and Stewart thinks it might interest you to learn more about the community, how it works, and maybe even get input from you."

"But I won't be an adult until I turn eighteen. I don't want to go."

"Adulthood is different here, and you're going. End of discussion."

A knock sounded on the door. Mom and Sapphira were still arguing and Eva was in the bathroom, so I answered the door and found Hannah with the four-year-old Tim in tow.

"Becky asked me to watch this little rascal this afternoon. There's a log playpen behind their trailer. We can play there until Mike and Becky get back. It will be fun," Hannah said.

"Okay, we have to wait for Eva, but then we can go."

I grabbed my trucks from the bedroom, yelling our plan at Eva through the bathroom door as I passed, and by the time I got back, Eva was getting her shoes on.

Thick logs, stacked two high and attached using bolts, formed a small square pen behind the blue trailer house a couple doors from ours.

"Darn, there's a mud puddle," said Hannah, pointing to the water pooled in the right corner. "I guess we can still play in here, but we need to make sure Tim stays clean."

The mud would be the perfect place to use my trucks, but since Tim wanted to play with them, too, I took them to the opposite side.

"We should play house," said Eva. "I'll be the daughter. Hannah, you should be the mom."

"I'm the puppy!" shouted Tim, who began running around, barking.

"What do you want to be, Sophia?" asked Hannah.

"I don't want to play, but you guys can."

I used my trucks to create a mound of dirt, patted it to form a cone, and decided it was a castle. It needed a moat, so I dug a trench and listened as the others played.

"Now, Eva, you're of age now," Hannah said, "So it's time to find your celestial husband. Usually one is provided for you by the leaders of the community, but I have the right to choose one for you. But first, we have to teach you how to be a good wife. Do you know what a good wife looks like?"

"No Mommy, will you tell me?" asked Eva, playing her role.

"Well, rule one is you have to start your period. That's when we know a girl becomes a woman and is ready to get married. Always remember, it's a very important job for a woman to have lots of babies. This is what grows our community family."

I glanced over my shoulder, wondering if I should try to get them to play something different. Their conversation made me feel sick to my stomach. Eva was too young to hear about this stuff. Tim ran around both of them, barking and trying to get their attention.

"Tim, be a good doggy and go lie down," said Eva, patting his head.

"Your grandpa told me this next tip when I was your age, and now it's your turn to learn it," continued Hannah. "Are you paying attention, Eva, or is the puppy being too much of a distraction?"

"I'm listening."

"Good, because boys become men at the age of fourteen, but that doesn't mean your husband will be young. You could get a husband as old as sixty-five. It all depends on who in the community can take care of a wife and children. Sometimes, a woman is married to a man who already has a wife, because he's the only man who can take care of her and—Tim, no!" shouted Hannah.

I turned in time to see Tim jump into the center of the puddle. Hannah covered her mouth with her hands and gasped.

Tim laughed and continued splashing. "I'm a puppy, taking a bath!"

"Stop, Tim, you'll be in so much trouble!" Hannah tried to get near him to pull him out, but every time she took a step toward him, he jumped again, and she moved back to avoid getting splattered with mud.

"What's going on over here?" came Richard's rough voice from behind me.

Tim froze at the harsh sound and cried.

"He wouldn't listen when I told him not to go near the puddle," Hannah said.

Richard climbed over the logs, grabbed Tim's arm and dragged him to the middle of the square. "I'll whip that disobedience right out of you, boy."

I watched in horror as he dug a crusty sock from his pocket, shoved it in Tim's mouth, and pushed him face-down on the ground.

Tim spit the sock out and tried to free himself from Richard's grasp, but Richard held both of Tim's arms behind his back and pinned him with a knee, stuffing the sock back into his mouth. Then he removed the paddle from his belt loop.

Thwack, thwack, thwack, thwack.

Eva stood next to me and I grabbed her arm, dragged her behind me into the corner farthest away from them and lifted her over the barrier. "Run, go back to the trailer, now."

I huddled in the corner as Richard pulled the sock from Tim's mouth and tied the paddle onto his belt loop.

Tim lay in the dirt and howled.

"Shut up, boy, or I'll whip you again," said Richard, standing menacingly over the small boy.

He's crazy! Eva and I have to get out of here before he uses that thing on us.

The little boy looked up at Richard with a terrified expression but didn't stop screaming.

"I'll get him quiet," Hannah said, stepping forward and holding her hands out toward Tim, who scrambled to his feet and buried his face in her shirt.

"Get yourselves cleaned up before your parents see this mess." Richard dusted himself off and left.

Hannah rocked Tim until he stopped crying. "I better get him back so we can clean up. I'll see you guys later."

I nodded and ran back to the trailer to check on Eva.

After dinner that night, I got drowsy like I had the evening before, the weight of my limbs pulling me into sleep. This didn't seem normal. Was I sick?

I woke up groggy the next morning, like you do when you take cold medicine, and told Mom and Sapphira about the numbing tiredness. I asked if they thought I was sick.

Sapphira felt my forehead. "You don't have a fever."

"Sophia, it's just the humidity here. Your body is working harder to breathe because of the moisture in the air. Plus, you've been playing outside, and that will make you tired."

The air *was* different here than in Utah, but I didn't have trouble breathing. Mom was convinced I wasn't coming down with anything, though, so I tried to stop worrying.

There was a knock at the door.

"Oh, you girls are hanging out at Hannah's house today. Eva, go let her in, please," said Mom.

Hannah had a huge smile on her face. "Are you guys ready to come hang out with me? Mom got us popcorn, Wheat Thins, and raisins for a special snack while we watch movies."

"Is it popcorn with extra butter?" asked Eva.

"No, Mom popped it on the stove in olive oil, so it's not even salty. It's so much better for you," said Hannah.

Eva and I looked at each other, and I knew we were thinking the same thing: *Gross.*

"Where are you going, Mom?" Eva asked.

"Sapphira and I are going into town."

"Why can't we go?" I asked.

"Yeah, we want to see the town too, you know," Eva added.

"You're cute," said Mom, "but you can't go this time."

My head was still foggy, and I wanted to lie down. I grabbed Eva's hand to stop any further comments from her. "Come on, it's been a while since we've been allowed to watch TV."

Mom and Sapphira walked over to Hannah's with us. When we arrived, Eva and Hannah ran inside, but I stayed back. "Mom, I don't feel good."

She kissed my forehead. "You'll be fine. Now, go enjoy your movie day."

Walking up the steps to Hannah's house, I overheard Sapphira tell Mom that Stewart made her uncomfortable.

Mom glanced my way, and I hurried inside but kept the door open a crack.

"Why does he make you uncomfortable?" she asked.

"He kept whispering in my ear during the meeting, saying I was young, beautiful, and pure."

"Come on, Sophia, the movie is starting," yelled Hannah.

I closed the door all the way before Hannah could catch me listening at the door and joined her and my little sister in the living room.

Chapter 5

9 Months Before The FBI standoff

Three weeks passed before Mom took me and Eva out of the small trailer park to town. We drove the ugly red-and-green truck to the smallest store I'd ever seen, to pick up groceries.

"Can we get cereal, Mom? Pleeease?" begged Eva.

"No, it goes against community rules."

"Ugh, we never get anything we like anymore." Eva folded her arms and sat on the floor by one of the cash registers.

For the past week, Eva had complained about everything. The trailer was too hot or too cold, her dolls were dirty, and she didn't like doing chores. I was afraid that, one of these days, Richard would hear and use the paddle on her.

"Let her be. She isn't harming anyone, and the store isn't busy, so she won't be in the way," said Mom.

I followed Mom around, trying to keep an eye on my little sister at the same time. Not an easy task.

"Why haven't we started school?" I asked, hoping Mom wouldn't scold me for asking questions when we were away from the others.

"I'm sure Stewart has his reasons for letting you kids have more free time. I wouldn't worry about it. Go find peanut butter while I wait for the turkey meat. Get the all-natural kind, with no added salt or sugar."

"Can I have a notebook for drawing? I saw some at the front for fifteen cents." I actually planned on using it as a journal to record all the strange stuff these people said and did.

"That's fine, but get the peanut butter, too."

After grabbing the requested item, I checked on Eva and got a notebook. I noticed a black man waiting in line at the register where my sister sat. When he finished buying his things, he bent over and said something to her. Eva bolted to her feet, her eyes wide, and she ran toward me.

"Are you okay? What did he say?" I asked.

"He asked why I was sad."

"Is that all? Why did you run away?"

"Edgar and Stewart told us not to talk to black people. And remember what Hannah said about them being dangerous?"

I remembered, but I didn't trust the people in the community. They said strange things, and I didn't believe what Hannah said about their skin color being a punishment from God. "I wouldn't believe everything Hannah says, Eva."

Back home, we helped Mom put the groceries away before going out to play. Eva told Hannah about her encounter with the black man and appeared satisfied with the fear and awe she showed at the telling. In this version, the man yelled at her and had a "huge knife in his belt."

Whenever Hannah and Eva insisted on playing the same old games or brought out their Barbie's, I left the trailer and wandered around, eventually ending up in my new favorite place, a tree near the big fire pit. The bark was white and it still had a lot of leaves on it to hide in. It looked like two trees growing from the same stump. One grew at an angle and had the perfect places to step so it was possible to climb high with little effort and remain unseen while observing the adults as they held their meetings. Most of what they said I didn't understand, but I listened anyway.

Today, things seemed quiet, so I pulled out a pocketknife I had found in the trailer a few days earlier. I used it to break off bark from the tree and to carve into the wood. The blade was dull, so it took effort and concentration to get it to do what I wanted.

I'd finished my initials when voices nearing the fire pit distracted me. I quickly shifted my body so I was better hidden.

"We got the money to get Edgar, but it's come at a price," said a man's voice that sounded like Tim's dad, Mike.

"What's the problem?" This voice sounded familiar, but I couldn't figure out where I'd heard it.

"Never mind that, we have to move." The third voice was Richard's.

"Everyone?" The second man let out a stream of curse words and I remembered the voices I'd heard when Hannah, Eva, and I were playing by the stream.

"Stop it, Sam. Yes, everyone. Jack's scouting a place in Louisiana. We need one before freeing Edgar. The community needs to be on the road when we go get him," Richard said.

My heart sank. Mom had told us he would return, but I'd hoped she was wrong. I'd be quite okay with it if I never saw him again.

"When will we announce it?" asked Mike.

"Jack should return on Friday or Saturday. We can announce on Sunday evening, then everyone can pack Monday and we can leave on Tuesday. If it doesn't work out, we'll hold off," said Richard.

The second guy, Sam, swore again. "I knew those girls would be trouble for us."

"Enough. That family is a blessing. The oldest is marrying age, the second isn't too far behind. If we want our community to grow, we need them," Richard said.

Sapphira? She wasn't old enough to marry! Who would she marry, anyway? There weren't any boys her age. Then I thought back to Hannah's words when she and Eva were playing house. I shuddered and hoped they would leave soon.

"Who's up there?" shouted Richard.

My heart pounded. I must have made a noise, or rattled the leaves ... The tree shook, and I realized someone was climbing up. I squeezed my eyes shut and pretended to be asleep.

A hand grabbed my ankle. "Hey, what are you doing up here?" Richard shook my leg so hard I was afraid I would fall and hugged the branch. "You little eavesdropping sinner. Climb down here now."

"No, I was asleep, I wasn't eavesdropping, I swear."

"Down outta this tree, pronto." Richard's head disappeared.

I scrambled down and saw the paddle in his hand.

"This isn't the first time you've snooped. Now, bend over. I'll teach you to listen in on adult conversations."

I stared at the paddle, then at the trailers, and tried to make out an escape route. Before I could bolt, Sam grabbed me and pushed me to the ground, pinning me there, with his knee digging into my back. His hand pressed my head into the dirt. I heard the *thwack* of the paddle and felt a sharp stinging pain on my backside.

Thwack, Thwack, Thwack.

Tears streamed from my eyes, and I screamed each time the paddle made contact. When it was over, Sam finally released me.

"A blessing, huh?" Sam spit near my face, and the three men walked away.

I lay there, crying, and tried to catch my breath. Pain radiated from my knees to the middle of my back. Would I even be able to stand? After a few minutes the pain dulled into a burning sensation, and I lifted myself off the ground with shaking arms. Dusting my clothes and wiping my eyes, I slowly made my way back to the trailer.

Mom, I thought, wouldn't stand for this. Maybe now we could go home, back to our normal lives, away from these horrible people.

Once inside, I got a drink of water and lay face-down on the couch. Eva was still at Hannah's, and Mom and Sapphira were not in the trailer. Perfect. Ten minutes later, I was still in pain and decided to see what Richard had done. I grabbed a stool, took it to the bathroom, and gently pulled down my pants and underwear, looking over my shoulder into the mirror.

My rear end was bright red, with small circles of pale pink here and there. I pulled my pants up and returned to the couch.

When Mom returned, I told her what happened and showed her the marks, which were still somewhat visible.

"Who did this to you?" she asked.

"Richard."

She hugged me and stroked my hair. "Oh, baby, I'm so sorry. I'll make sure he never touches you again. Don't worry. I am the only person who has any right to punish you, and I'll make sure Richard knows it."

Chapter 6

Sunday, the day I hated most, arrived. They forced us to be part of their Sunday rituals. We had to sit around the big fire pit and listen to Hannah's dad, Stewart, who loved to talk. It was the only time his eyes had any life in them. It was like going to the Mormon Church ward, except there was no Sunday school for the kids, and it lasted four hours.

Stewart always spent the first forty-five minutes lecturing Eva, Sapphira, and me about forgetting everything we used to know about our life outside the community, and reminding us of the rules. I spent the time daydreaming; wishing I could be home with my dog, or in my room, where I could shut the door. I hated that Stewart tried to make us forget, so I made myself remember.

After church we weren't allowed to do anything. At first we could read books, but Stewart took that option away after he discovered me and Hannah helping Eva with the harder words.

"No more reading on Sundays. It requires too much work to help you, Eva," he said. "This is a day of rest, and I won't let you be a stumbling block to your sister and my daughter."

So, we usually ended up at Hannah's watching cartoons. I would much rather have played outside with my trucks, but since they were toys based on real-life working vehicles, it went against the rules.

We even had to make enough meals on Saturday to last the rest of the weekend, because apparently making a peanut butter sandwich was hard work. It was fine, though. I really enjoyed the chance to spend time with Mom, even if we didn't talk much. It was the only day of the week I got to spend any time with her, and it was comforting to have her near.

The Sunday following my spanking, Jack was in the crowd and I waited for the announcement about the move. It never came, and they released us kids. I felt a wave of relief. I would have more time to convince Mom to take us home. She never told me if she had talked to Richard about hitting me, but it didn't matter. Since Mom was never around, I knew I couldn't trust him not to do it again.

"Girls, Edgar is joining us again soon," Mom announced that evening, as she placed one of the peanut butter and jelly sandwiches we'd made together in front of me.

My heart dropped. *They must have waited until we left to announce the move. Not fair.*

She sat with us and continued. "Tomorrow, we leave here and head somewhere else for a while. Stewart believes God told him where we should move. After you eat, pack as much as you can tonight, then in the morning take your bags to the truck. It will make the move go much faster."

"Do we have to, Mama?" Eva asked, around a mouthful of food. "I like it here."

"I know, sweetie, we move when we are told. It will be best for us, and I'm sure you'll like the next place even more."

"Is Hannah going to move, too?"

"Yes, Eva, everyone is moving."

I finished eating, then sat on the couch near Sapphira, who was reading a book.

"Sapphira? Can I snuggle with you?" I whispered.

"Sure, come on over."

Scooting over, I wrapped my arms around her, and she wrapped one arm around me, the other still holding her book.

"I don't want to move," I whispered.

"I know."

"Why can't we go home?"

"You know why," said Sapphira.

"Remind me."

She sighed. "Mom married Edgar, and these are Edgar's … people."

"But they aren't family."

"No. Now hush, I'm trying to read."

"Okay. Sapphira?"

"What?"

"I've missed you. I wish you didn't have to be with the adults."

She sighed again, but I noticed it was more drawn-out and shaky this time. "Me, too."

The next morning we were up before the sun to finish loading our things into the truck. We were among the first to finish, and as the sky lightened, my family sat waiting in the ugly two-toned vehicle. I could see Richard moving from car to car, talking to each driver. When he reached us, I stared out the opposite window to avoid eye contact with him.

"I'm going to send people out. You'll be the last to leave and will follow Stewart and Lindsey. That way, if you're stopped for any reason you can tell the police you're on a vacation with your sister and her family. As soon as they're ready, you guys will head out," said Richard.

"Okay, thank you."

The three vehicles in front of us drove away. Hannah's family must have slept in late, because, even when the others had gone, we waited a long time. Which, if anyone had bothered to ask me, did not seem in keeping with their own rules of setting a good example for the rest of the community. I pulled out my notebook and wrote about this observation.

"Maybe we should go help," suggested Sapphira.

I elbowed her and shook my head. All I wanted to do was finish writing and go back to sleep.

"Go see how much they have left. If it's a lot, come and get Sophia and Eva to help," said Mom.

I rolled my eyes and leaned my head against the window.

Sapphira climbed out and returned a few minutes later. "Lindsey said they're done and they're just checking their trailer one more time for anything they might have missed."

Mom nodded. I could tell she was irritated. She hated waiting for people.

A few minutes later, Stewart walked up to us, shouting over his shoulder. "Good heavens, woman, it's time you lose weight. We're an hour past the time we should have left." He leaned in through Mom's window, flashing Sapphira a creepy grin. "We're ready to go. I just need to pull the car around, and you can follow us out."

"Mom, do we get to go to Utah to see Daddy now?" Eva asked.

Stewart pointed at her. "You need to forget about your dad, young lady. Edgar is your dad now. Say it. Say: 'Edgar is my dad.'"

Eva's bottom lip trembled. "Edgar is my dad."

"Good girl. Let's head out."

I wrapped my arm around my little sister after Stewart walked away. "Edgar is not your daddy," I whispered to her. I refused to let either of us forget.

This trip wasn't as long as the one that took us to the trailer park. We arrived at our new living place by midday and parked alongside the others near a big red barn.

I got out of the car and craned my neck to take in the surroundings. There were fields in every direction. Near the barn stood a white house with big, old trees around it and railroad tracks behind it.

Walking toward the house, I took in the details. A wide porch covered the width of the house and had two wooden rocking chairs on it. We entered through a screen door, and I jumped as it slammed behind us. A tall, skinny woman with curly blond hair and brown eyes stood in the entrance. She looked to be about Mom's age, maybe a little older.

"Welcome to our little slice of heaven in Louisiana, y'all. I'm Carol. My husband George is out doin' somethin' or another so you'll meet him later. Now, let me show you where y'all will be stayin' so you can get settled."

Her accent fascinated me.

"Sapphira, my oldest, will stay with me," Mom said. "If that's not too much trouble."

"Not at all. I'll show the younger ones their room upstairs and be right back to take care of y'all."

"Tim is staying with me and Mike," said Becky. "If that's okay with you, Carol."

"That will be perfect."

Eva clung to Sapphira's arm. "I want you to stay with us," she whined.

"Don't be rude, Eva. Do as you're told and follow this nice lady to your room," Sapphira scolded.

Eva made a pouty face but obeyed. Hannah joined us as we followed Carol up a narrow, creaky staircase to a short hallway with two doors, one on each side. She took us into the one on the right.

"You will sleep up here. The other room is storage, not a place for kids. Please excuse me. I need to show the others where they'll be staying."

I looked around. The ceiling made the room look like a large triangle, with the walls sloping inward at an angle. A small, round window was the only natural light we would have. A bare bulb with a pull string attached to it hung on the wall to the left of the window. Three mattresses lay on the floor, lined up next to each other, with blankets folded on top. The rest of the room was bare. No pictures on the walls, shelves, or even a closet where we could put our clothes.

"I call the middle," Eva said, tossing her luggage onto the middle mattress.

"This side is mine," said Hannah, indicating the mattress farthest from the window.

"Okay, I'll take this one." I sat down on my mattress and fingered the blanket. It was thick and looked homemade, like the ones at Grandma's house back home. *I wonder if I'll ever see her or those blankets again.*

"Let's go explore," I said to the other two.

We left our things and headed back downstairs. At the bottom of the stairs and to the right lay a large kitchen. To the left was the living room. I went into the living room to explore. It had smooth, shiny hardwood flooring. In one corner was a large, black, wood-burning fireplace that sat on big flat rocks. On the opposite side of the room was a hallway with several doors on each side of it.

"Stop," said Richard, who was coming in through the screen door as I reached the middle of the room. "Where do you think you're going?"

"To find my mom." I glared at him.

"You're only allowed upstairs or outside; the rest of the house is off-limits. Got it?"

I crossed my arms. "I have to ask her a question."

He bent over so his head was even with mine. "And what question is that? I'm sure I can answer it for you."

Since I had nothing to ask her, I said the first thing that popped into my head. "I need to get the truck keys."

"The locks on your truck are broken, and your mom is outside."

I broke eye contact with Richard and headed for the front door without a word.

"Hey," he barked.

I checked my steps, but didn't look back.

"Upstairs or outside—that's it."

Outside, I found Mom and Sapphira. "Do we have sheets?" I asked her. "There aren't any on the beds. Also, how are we supposed to stay warm? The blankets on our beds have holes in them."

"There are no extra blankets, but you have your sleeping bags. If you girls get cold, then snuggle close to stay warm," she said.

"Mom and I are sleeping on cots wherever there's room," Sapphira put in. "I don't think they expect us to be here long."

"If there's not enough room downstairs, why doesn't Sapphira sleep with us?"

"Sapphira isn't a child anymore, so she will stay with the rest of the adults," Mom snapped.

Since Sapphira was only fourteen, it felt more like the object was to keep her away from me.

After the vehicles were unloaded, Mom instructed Hannah, Eva and I to play outside until dinner time, but said we had to stay within shouting distance of the house. We tried a game of tag, but with only three of us, that got boring pretty fast.

The other two pulled out their dolls, and I took that as an opportunity to explore. As I had noticed before, grassy fields and open spaces surrounded us. This made me feel very exposed, and I desperately missed my tree at the other location. I wandered toward the back of the house, where I spotted what must have been a small vegetable garden, but now the growing season was over and everything was dead.

I noticed the door to the barn was open a crack, so I walked over and quickly slipped in. Inside was a row of stalls that contained four horses. I made my way to the closest one and stuck my hand through the wooden slats. The horse was brown with a white spot on its forehead. It sniffed my fingers, but didn't come close enough for me to pet it. I moved down the walkway. The second horse was mostly white, with gray spots on its backside. That one stuck its head over the door to the stall and let me scratch its nose. It also tried to eat my hair, which made me giggle. I kissed its velvety nose before checking in on the other two. The third was black all over and appeared to be sleeping, and the fourth was another brown horse, with a long white stripe on its nose instead of a spot. This one stuck its head out, too, but when I reached out, it pulled away from me, startled.

The white horse instantly became my favorite, and I wandered back to it and scratched its head for a while. I looked around the barn, taking in all the saddles, blankets, tools, and other items stored there before greeting each of the large animals again.

The brown horse with the white stripe was finally warming up to me when the barn door opened, and the horse shied away again. I jumped, pulling my hand away. A man with a cowboy hat stood in the doorway, peering at me.

"Well, you must be the fourth kiddo staying with us," he said.

"Yes, sir. I love your horses," I said quietly.

"Yeah, they are lovable. Those your sisters out there playing with dolls?"

"The younger one, the other is a friend," I said.

"I'm George, Carol's husband." He said in welcome.

"Sophia," I muttered, scuffing the toe of my shoe in the dirt of the floor.

"So, which of these horses do you like best?" He asked.

"I like the white one best." I smiled and looked toward my new friend.

George laughed. "That's Dakota. She's the youngest of the bunch and likes to cause trouble. I'm sure you're just a curious girl, but the barn isn't the best place for a young person to be alone. Next time, make sure you get permission. Deal?"

I smiled. George was the first adult I'd met since we left home that I liked. "Deal," I said, and held out my hand for him to shake.

He laughed again and shook my hand. "Now, get on out of here before my wife finds you."

I ran outside into the fading sunshine. Eva and Hannah were still playing dolls on the lawn in front of the house, so I wandered over to the railroad tracks and balanced on the metal rails. About thirty minutes later, I heard Carol's voice calling everyone for dinner.

Smoke curled from a barbecue grill nearby and a long, folding table was set up near the back door. It held paper plates, napkins, plastic cups, fixings for hamburgers and hot dogs, and two different salads.

Eva and Hannah waited in line to get their food. I walked over and joined them just as Stewart appeared.

"Girls, I'm sure you're hungry, but you were selfish while everyone did the work of setting up, so you can be the last to get your food. And while you're eating, I want to go over the rules while we're here."

Tears formed in my little sister's eyes, and I pulled her into a hug. "Come on, it won't be too much longer."

Sitting on the steps of the back porch, we watched the adults get their food and find places at the four wooden picnic tables. Finally, no one else was in line and we got up to get our food. Stewart stopped us again.

"Girls, George hasn't gotten his plate yet. He's been busy cooking on the grill. When he's done, then you can get yours."

I wanted to punch him.

A few minutes later, George piled the last of the hamburgers and hot dogs onto a tray and placed them on the table, then helped himself to the food. The three of us looked at Stewart and he nodded. We filled our plates with what remained and sat at the table across from Stewart.

"The Holy Scriptures tell us the first will be last and the last first, and you girls got a lesson on that today. Tomorrow, you will join us for morning prayers. After breakfast, you'll find out what your chores are from Carol and George, and you'll do them every day except Sunday. When you finish those, you can have play time outside until you're called for. Then you will remain upstairs for the rest of the night," said Stewart.

We nodded in unison, stuffing our faces and only half listening. It was all I could do to not tell him off.

"Good." Stewart left and walked up to Lindsey, who was putting a hamburger together. "What are you doing, wife?" he asked, rudely knocking the plate out of her hands.

"It's not for me, I was—" She backed away from him.

"You know obesity is a sin. We've prayed about it together, and what did the Lord tell me about what you should eat, wife?"

Lindsey's face grew red, and she stared at the ground. "Lettuce with lemon juice."

"Clean up this mess," Stewart said, walking away and taking a seat next to Sapphira.

Lindsey knelt down and picked up the ruined sandwich, then filled another plate with lettuce and sat at an empty table with her back toward everyone.

What is wrong with these people? How could he treat his wife that way in front of everyone? I hated Stewart.

Chapter 7

The prayer session would require us to sit still with our hands stretched into the air for an hour. As I walked in, I noticed in dismay that Edgar was sitting next to Mom. He must have arrived late the previous night, because he hadn't been at dinner.

I pushed my growing dread aside and spent most of the prayer time trying to keep Eva from getting into trouble. All she did was groan and squirm. Eventually, she stopped doing both and simply fell asleep on my shoulder. Except for the occasional glance from Stewart or Richard, we were ignored.

My arms grew tired within a few minutes, and when Eva fell asleep, I couldn't keep them up anymore. No one explained why we had to do this. I thought it was stupid. And why were Sapphira and Becky sitting on silky purple pillows? *Is this national sit-on-a-pillow day or something? Could this morning get any weirder?*

Stewart led the prayer but kept repeating himself and used strange words I didn't understand, like "thee" and "thou." I kept my focus on Eva, but one thing he said caught my attention.

"God, we humble ourselves and come to thee, that thee might show us where paradise is. Thee have spoken to thine children and directed us to leave the evil and corrupt society behind and begin a new community that follows thy laws and thy will. Show us where this paradise is. Lead us to the place of thy light so we might live according to thy will forevermore."

Paradise? Light? The words brought back a memory of what I'd experienced after my accident two years ago. The pure white light that had surrounded me. Is that what they were talking about? If so, why didn't I feel the same way around them as I did standing in that light? Was it because they were searching, too? Why could I sense it and not them?

Mike was shaking my arm, pulling me away from the memory. "You girls need to go find Carol and George for your chores." It was only then that I realized the couple hadn't been there for prayer.

We found them in the barn.

"Good morning. I hear you girls are great helpers. Is that true?" asked Carol.

"We sure are!" I said, a little too enthusiastically. I was sure they wouldn't get my sarcasm.

Carol smiled. "Good, George and I have to go exercise the horses and check the fences. While we're gone, you girls can clean out the stalls."

I slumped in disappointment. I had hoped we would get to interact with the horses, but no, we only got to clean up their poop.

George took us to one stall and grabbed a pitchfork. "Now, you want to make sure you're getting under the manure and not stabbing it, otherwise you'll have a sticky mess on your pitchfork. Like this." He demonstrated.

I didn't know there was so much to learn about picking up poop. Back home, whenever we had to pick up dog poo, we used a shovel. I couldn't image horse poo being much different.

"Not much to it, think you gals can—" He broke off abruptly. "Watch out, little miss, you'll step in—"

"Ewww!" Eva screamed.

I whirled around to find her standing in the middle of a poop pile, and busted out laughing.

"Get it off, get it off, get if off!" she yelled as she dragged her foot through the hay, but that only coated her shoe with straw.

"Hold still, little miss, we'll get you squared away," George exclaimed, running to her.

But Eva didn't stop, until she tripped and fell backwards, landing bum-first in the pile of poop she'd just stepped in.

I doubled over in laughter and couldn't catch my breath.

Eva started crying, "It's not funny!"

George turned away, his shoulders heaving in barely suppressed laughter.

Carol stepped forward and lifted Eva to her feet. She was the only one, other than Eva, not laughing. In fact, she looked irritated by the whole scene. "Come on, let's get you hosed off while George shows Sophia and Hannah the rest of your chores." Carol gave George an irritated look before leading Eva out of the barn.

After we had all collected ourselves, George showed us where the extra straw was, which we were to lay down once we cleaned the stalls.

As soon as he finished, I raced outside to check on Eva. She stood in front of the barn, angry and wet, arms folded. I walked up to her, trying to keep a straight face, and gave her a hug. "It will be okay," I said.

"Now, if you finish before we get back, fill up their water troughs with the hose. Don't worry about feeding them, we'll do that when we return," added Carol, and they took the four horses and left.

Eva was too small for the pitchfork, and the wheelbarrow was too heavy, which left most of the work to me and Hannah. That was fine with me, since Eva was still wet and cried whenever any task felt too difficult for her.

We switched off picking up the horse poo until we got to the second stall. Then I took over, and Eva and Hannah wheeled the manure to the dump pile. Carol and George came back as we were spreading fresh straw in the last stall.

"Good work, girls," said George. "This will be your chore every morning. There are soap and towels in back. Wash yourselves up and you can go play."

"Can I pet the horses, George?" I asked, putting the pitchfork away.

"You girls will stay away from the horses and the barn at all times except in the mornings when you clean their stalls. Understood?" said Carol sharply.

I headed to the back to wash my hands and secretly rolled my eyes. "Yes, I understand."

For the rest of the morning, Eva, Hannah and I walked along a little stream we found, and balanced on the railroad tracks. We made up a game where we had to jump from one railroad tie to another, and the rocks between were lava.

Jack found us a few minutes into our game. "Girls, it's not safe out here. A train might come through and squish you." He motioned for us to get off the tracks. "I'll show you a trick, but only if you promise not to come back out here."

We promised. Jack walked up to the metal rails and knelt, putting his ear to the track. "If you put your ear to the rail, you'll feel the vibration of an approaching train." He motioned us over and let us try, but there was no vibration. I wanted to wait until a train came by, but Jack wouldn't allow that, so we headed back toward the house and did somersaults in the yard.

Sapphira came outside holding the silky pillow. She placed it on one of the porch steps and sat on it. I took a break from practicing handstands and sat next to her. Up close I could see the pillow had white lace and silver sequins on the edges.

"You shouldn't sit with me, Sophia," she said. She kept glancing back at the house, as if to make sure no one would see me with her.

"Why not?" Her dismissal hurt.

"Because I'm on my period, which makes me unclean," she whispered, and red splotches appeared on her cheeks.

"So? What does that matter? Is that why you're sitting on that stupid pillow?"

Sapphira leaned toward me. "Stop asking so many questions. You'll find out soon enough. Now go away and leave me alone."

"What is the big deal about asking questions? I just want to know what's going on."

The older girls at school had talked about their periods in the bathrooms, but none of them ever said they had to sit on a pillow. I was so confused, but also determined. I could tell something was bothering Sapphira, so unless someone forced me to leave, I would stay with my big sister.

"You don't want to know. Now please, go away." Sapphira buried her face in her hands.

Becky popped her head out the door. "Sapphira, Stewart wants to speak with you."

Sapphira got up, grabbed her pillow and headed inside.

"Becky, do you have a minute? I have a question," I said.

"You can ask. I can't guarantee an answer," said Becky, who was standing half in and half out of the door.

"Sapphira told me she had to sit on that purple pillow because she was on her period. What does that mean?"

Becky smiled and came out on the front porch. "How old are you now?"

"I'm going to be ten in a few months."

"Ten, huh? I suppose you're old enough to know. Do you know why women have their periods?"

I shrugged. "I know it's when girls get boobs."

Becky laughed. "Here we call them breasts, but never in front of the men, it's more proper. But you're correct. It also signals that a girl is ready to have children. Every time you have a period, it means a baby doesn't get to live. The pillow is holy and catches the souls of the unborn children who never get to live on Earth because the woman didn't get pregnant. Does that make sense?"

Actually, it sounded crazy, so I ignored her question and asked, "What happens to all the souls trapped in the pillow?"

"When the bleeding stops, the woman cleans herself and prays over the pillow to release the soul or souls back to heaven, where they can have another chance in another woman."

The image of a ghost baby covered in blood being transferred to another person's body passed through my mind, and my stomach churned. "That sounds pretty gross."

"That's why women are considered unclean and have to sit away from everyone else while on their monthly cycle, and since men can be dense sometimes, the pillow is a reminder for them to stay away,

too. I have to go back inside and get Tim down for his nap. If you
have more questions we can talk later," she said, standing up again.

Monthly cycle? I hope I never have to have that, I thought as she
walked away.

Chapter 8

Almost two weeks after arriving at Carol and George's house, I noticed Mom wasn't showing up at prayer or any of the family meals. Eva didn't seem bothered by it, until bedtime, when Mom didn't come to say goodnight. I tried to comfort her, but my mind swam with "what-ifs" and I quickly tired of her whining. I had to find Sapphira; she was the only person I trusted to tell me the truth. I crept downstairs and found her in the living room, sitting next to Stewart. Trying to talk to her now was out of the question. I crept back to bed. I'd have to keep my eyes open for an opportunity.

Five days passed with no chance to talk to my big sister, and Mom still hadn't appeared. Desperate, I asked Carol if she had seen her when we went out to do our chores.

"No, I've been very busy. If she's not in the house, she must have had an errand to run."

She didn't make eye contact with me and seemed nervous. I thought it strange the owner of the house didn't know where one of her guests had gone.

At mealtimes, the kids sat at their own table and the men took turns babysitting us. Tonight was Edgar's turn. Without acknowledging any of us, he sat down and ate.

"Where's my mom?" I asked, watching to see if he would at least look at me. He didn't.

"Yeah, is she coming back? I miss her," Eva chimed in.

"Your mom is fine, girls." The tone of his voice told me I should drop the subject. But I decided to push him a little. After all, this was my mom we were talking about. If she left, we'd be stuck with Edgar forever.

"Can we see her before bed tonight?" I asked.

Lifting his eyes our direction he said shortly, "No. Now eat your supper."

It wasn't unusual for him to be silent when he watched us, but there was still something suspicious about the way he was acting.

The next day, they told us to stay upstairs until someone came to get us. Carol brought up a bunch of board games, books, and a tray of snacks and juice, which meant we were probably stuck up here all day. I took it as a sign they were trying to keep the truth of my mom's whereabouts away from me and Eva.

We started off with a game of Go Fish.

"I don't want to play anymore. I'm sleepy," said Eva, ten minutes into our game.

"Me too," said Hannah.

I furrowed my brow. "Me too."

It was just like at the trailer park, when I thought I was getting sick but Mom insisted I wasn't. My thoughts raced. If the tiredness wasn't caused by an illness, but we all had it … a knot formed in my stomach. I had to find Mom, now.

I got up and headed toward the stairs, but a wave of dizziness hit me and I stumbled and fell to my knees. The tiredness took over and it took all I had to crawl back to my mattress. I would just sleep for a moment, then find her.

Noise from downstairs startled me from the black nothing, and for a moment, I couldn't remember where I was. The angled ceiling with the bare bulb, the wooden floor, the small window, the row of mattresses—none of it looked familiar in my disoriented state. Sweeping my eyes across the room, I spotted Eva sprawled on her bed.

Then it all came flooding back, and I was pretty sure this was the real nightmare. Mom was missing, and we were not at home, not safe.

I scrambled to my feet and the room spun. The sun had set. *What was in that food?*

When the room finally stopped wobbling, I made my way downstairs carefully. Voices got louder and pots and pans rattled.

Standing in the doorway of the kitchen, I watched as the women cooked. The kitchen was not as big as the one at my house in Utah. It had a stove against the outer wall, with a window above it. The sink and counter were opposite the stove, with cupboards above and below.

"Well, look who decided to join the land of the living," said Lindsey. "I went up there at lunch and all you lazy pants were fast asleep. Are the other two awake?"

I shook my head, which sent the room spinning again.

Lindsey popped a piece of tomato into her mouth. "Dinner is almost ready. Please wake the other two. I don't want them sneaking food in the middle of the night, especially your little sister."

Heading back upstairs, I wondered how I could find Mom. I found both girls sitting, groggy-eyed, on their mattresses. "It's time to eat. Come on." I motioned to them before slowly going down the steps again.

"Sit at the table and I'll make a plate for you," said Lindsey when I reappeared.

A few minutes later, Hannah walked in, followed closely by Eva. "Did we really sleep all day?" Hannah asked.

Carol looked up from stirring a big pot of something that smelled like stew. "Sickness has been spreading. I hope you girls aren't catching it."

I noticed she gave Becky and Lindsey a strange look before turning back to her pan. I was confused by what she'd said, since Mom had told me the tiredness wasn't sickness.

Lindsey set a bowl of stew in front of us. Eva immediately began shoving spoonfuls into her mouth, but Hannah said a short prayer and placed a napkin on her lap before delicately eating.

I stared at my bowl of stew in disgust. Would I get tired again after eating this? My stomach growled, demanding me to quit being suspicious and eat. I ate slowly, watching everyone around me. Afterward, Lindsey put us to work cleaning, then sent us back to our room.

My mind still cloudy, I lay on my bed thinking about how I could find Mom. She'd now been missing six days, and I was beginning to think I would never see her again.

At prayer on the seventh day, Sapphira was acting strange. She looked uncomfortable, and Stewart wouldn't leave her side. At one point he reached over to hold her hand. Sapphira cringed but didn't pull away. I saw tears on her face, which made me clench my fists.

I knew now I had to find out where they were hiding Mom, and if finding a way to talk to Sapphira was out of the question, I was going to have to take matters into my own hands.

The perfect plan came to my mind. Since Carol had suggested we might be sick, why not play along? Who would be the easiest to convince? *Becky, I think.*

Walking up to her after prayer, I said, "I don't feel good," in the saddest voice I could muster.

"Hmm, you are a little warm," Becky said after placing her hand on my forehead. "Come with me and I'll get you some medicine."

I gave her my best puppy-dog eyes. "Can I see my mom?"

"No, honey, your mom is sick, too." She pulled a bottle of purple liquid out of a cabinet in the bathroom.

"Why didn't anyone tell me that? Everyone keeps telling me they don't know where she is," I said, still trying to sound pathetic.

"We are keeping her in a separate room so she doesn't get everyone else sick. Now, take this." She poured the syrup into the plastic cup that came with the bottle and handed it to me.

"No, I don't want that, I want my mom." Shoving the little cup away, I ran upstairs. Hot, angry tears streamed down my face. I was tired of everyone lying to me. Why were they keeping our mother from us? I wiped my face across the sleeve of my shirt and paced around the room. They would *not* keep her from us any longer.

Determined, I ran down the stairs, pushing past a shocked Becky, who had apparently followed me. The creaky wooden planks complained under my stomping footsteps. Everyone in the house could probably hear me, but I didn't care.

"Where do you think you're going? This space is off-limits to children," said Stewart, who was still sitting next to my sister as I rushed through the living room.

I ignored him. Now I was in the hallway, and I flung open every door as I ran down it, looking quickly into each room. Most were empty, but occasionally I was met with a startled look and a scolding word. I ignored those too, and kept up my search.

Finally, I reached the end of the hall and the last door. I heard voices and tried the handle. Locked. Several adults made their way toward me, so I pounded on the door. They would not keep me from my Mom. I planted my feet in case they tried to drag me away and continued slamming my fist against the wood panels. "Mom, Mom, are you in there?" I shouted.

Richard reached for me as the door opened, and I twisted away from his hand and pushed into the room. Mom lay on a bed, soaking wet with sweat.

"Baby," she said in a hoarse voice and reached for me.

Edgar and Lindsey were both in the room. I ran to Mom before they could stop me and hugged her. "What's wrong? Why wouldn't anyone tell us where you were?"

She stroked my hair. "I've been sick, that's all."

"That girl deserves a paddling for running through the house causing chaos. She doesn't belong back here," said Richard, who still stood in the doorway.

"You won't touch my girls," said Mom, trying to sit up.

Lindsey put a hand on Mom's shoulder. "Lie back down, you're still too weak to get up."

"These girls are never going to learn their place in the community if you try to keep them all to yourself," Richard said.

I ignored him and buried my head into Mom's shoulder. "No one would tell us where you were." A sob escaped me.

"You'll mind your business, Richard. What did you expect by keeping them from seeing me?" asked Mom.

Richard started to speak, but Edgar's voice cut through his complaints. "Let the girl see that her mother is all right."

Richard swore, and his heavy footsteps retreated.

I straightened and inspected Mom. A sweaty shine covered all of her visible skin, including her hands. Her hair was wet and stuck to her face and neck. I had never seen Mom like this before, and it scared me. "Are you going to get better? Should I call Dad and have him bring you some medicine?"

"I'm right here, and she's been getting everything she needs," said Edgar.

I rolled my eyes. "A real dad would have told me what was going on."

Mom smiled weakly. "I'm fine. All this sweat means I broke the fever I had. That's a good thing."

"I'll stay and help take care of you," I insisted stubbornly.

Mom shook her head. "No. I'll be up again in a couple of days. I want you to do what you're told. Keep doing your chores and take care of Eva. Now, please go, I'm tired."

I could tell the words took effort and moved to go, but then turned and impulsively gave her another hug before leaving.

The following day, things were back to normal. The heavy tiredness didn't return, and we sat through prayer, cleaned the stalls in the barn, and played until dark. In spite of my continued worry for Mom, I felt triumphant. These people had tried to keep me from her, and I won. There had been no punishment, and no harsh words from anyone after I left Mom's side, and it made me feel a bit invincible.

I rewarded myself by sneaking into the barn to scratch Dakota's nose and give her a handful of oats.

Chapter 9

8 Months Before The FBI Standoff

After Mom got well, George and Carol seemed to be observing the group more closely. It was obvious they weren't happy. Carol was much quieter and less friendly, and George kept closer to the house.

Our chores were still the same, but now only Carol took the horses. While the adults had their afternoon meeting, I took advantage of George's absence from the barn and headed out, making sure the other two girls didn't follow. I needed some alone time with Dakota. At the barn I looked around once more, opened the door just enough to slip through, and closed it quickly behind me. I looked around to make doubly sure George and Carol really weren't there, then grabbed a handful of oats from the bag and walked around to Dakota's stall.

"Hi again." I clicked my tongue and held my hand out to entice the horse to come over. She was being stubborn today, but I kept at it until she lazily made her way over to claim her gift.

I pulled the oats away and scratched her velvety nose, hoping she would put her big head over the wooden planks. She was hesitant at first, but the oats won her over. I giggled as the horse scooped the oats into her mouth with her lips. The barn door creaked open. I froze. *Busted.*

"What are you doing in here? What are you feeding her?" demanded Carol, taking quick steps toward me. I dropped my hand and the remaining oats scattered on the floor.

"Oats, from the bag back there," I replied defensively, pointing in the general direction of the oat bag.

Carol slapped my outstretched hand.

"Ow!" A red mark appeared on the spot.

"We told you to stay away from the horses. How dare you come in here and mess with my animals," she yelled, shaking her finger in my face. "Get out of here. Get out now, and don't come near this barn again, or I'll have you whipped, you hear me?"

I ran, tears streaming down my face. The thought of encountering Richard's paddle again was terrifying. Instead of running to the house, I ran toward the railroad tracks and sat on a rock surrounded by tall grass.

I heard Carol screaming for George. She seemed to get closer to my hiding place, and I peeked through the grass. She was about ten feet away and her face was bright red. I held my breath and tried to make myself as small as possible. George ran out of the house toward her.

"What's wrong? What happened?" he asked, reaching her and folding her into his arms.

"I can't take this anymore," cried Carol, pulling away from George's grasp.

"I want that crazy man and his people out of our house. That little girl was feeding Dakota. Who knows what strange ideas they've put in her head. What if she poisoned the oats?"

George glanced at the house, then rested his hands on her shoulders. "Calm down. Remember, we have a plan. Two more days and it will all be over, but we have to be careful. We don't want them to figure out what we've done."

Carol nodded and hugged George. "I'm sorry, I just can't bear to see those kids treated so poorly."

"I know, I know," said George, patting Carol on the back. He led her back toward the barn and they disappeared inside.

When the coast was clear, and I was sure no one would chase after me, I left my hiding spot and walked in the grass beside the railroad tracks. Despite having been told not to, I went here whenever I could get away from Hannah and Eva.

Now and then, I glanced back at the house, but no one came for me. I followed the tracks farther than I had before and wondered how far I could go before anyone came looking. After a while, I started to relax. The grass got taller and I knelt down and put my ear to the track—no vibration. I pretended to be on an African safari, hunting lions, until I discovered a train spike lying on the rocks. I inspected it, tried to pound it into the ground with a rock, and eventually decided to keep it as a treasure.

Once I was certain the coast was clear, I walked cautiously up to the house, looking through the windows to see that preparations for dinner had started. I knew if any adult saw my awesome find they would take it, so I stuck it in my pocket before jogging upstairs to hide it in my suitcase.

Dinner was uneventful, but I expected someone to scold me and didn't feel safe until after Mom came upstairs to say goodnight to us. She kissed my forehead before reaching over to tuck in Eva. "Girls, we're moving again in the morning. Stewart had a vision. He believes it's no longer safe for us here."

I relaxed. No reprimand from Mom. Carol hadn't said anything. I felt a pang of guilt for my disobedience toward George and his wife. They'd been kind to us.

Eva sighed. "Why do we always have to move just when I'm getting used to a place?"

Mom laughed. "I'm sure we'll find a permanent place soon."

"Where are we moving?" I asked.

Mom smoothed my hair away from my face. "I'm not sure. Jack is in charge of that. He left this morning and returned a few minutes ago, so I'll find out soon." She stood up, blew us a kiss and turned out the light as she left.

The following day, we packed our things into the ugly truck and were on the road by nine. Edgar was with us, and the whole group stayed together.

I slept for most of the trip, but for the first hour I talked to Sapphira. Or, at least I tried to. She said little but seemed happy to listen to Eva and me talk about our adventures on the farm. The only time I'd seen her in the last month was during prayer and meal times, and the one time she sat on the porch. Any time we tried to talk, someone would interrupt us or call Sapphira to another room. I missed her.

When I woke, Edgar had just parked the truck. I noticed the time on the dash said 1:30. The landscape was once again unfamiliar. Tall, skinny pine trees surrounded us, dotted with other types of trees with colorful leaves.

We followed Mom to several camping tents set up in a small, sandy area. Nearby a sign read "Frogs Land Hotel." Several yards from the tents lay a river. The water was green and had trees growing out of it.

Jack gathered everyone together.

"Okay everyone, we have a great opportunity here. I've made a deal with the hotel that owns all this property. We can stay in these tents for free while we do maintenance and cleaning work in the hotel. I know some of you are still working on painting billboard signs, so you'll be the exception.

"Each family unit will have their own tent, with some exceptions. Stewart will use the host camper trailer as a place to pray, study, hold meetings, and for his own personal use. The other camp trailer will be used for meetings and will be lived in and taken care of by Sapphira. Lindsey and Hannah will stay in a tent. Eva and Sophia will have their own tent. All other information will be communicated to you at the evening meeting."

After Jack's speech, he showed us our tents. I was excited to have Mom nearby, but wished Sapphira could be close too. Unloading the car was my only opportunity to talk to her, and I took it.

"I was hoping we would have a tent near each other, but it's cool you get to stay in your own trailer. Especially since I know you don't like camping. I bet Eva will be jealous," I said, walking alongside her.

Sapphira looked at her bags, her cheeks turning red. "It's not that cool. I don't have a choice where I stay. I just do what I'm told," she said, walking faster as we neared her trailer. She opened the door, stepped in, and turned back to me, her shoulders slumped. "I love you, Soph," she said and shut the door.

Chapter 10

"Why don't we stop there for now. I can see this is hard on you," said Stacy.

We'd been talking for two hours, and recalling all this was taking its toll, dredging up details I had tried hard to forget for years.

"I'm sorry. This part of the story brings up a lot of bad memories. I'll be okay in a minute."

Stacy handed me a bottle of water.

"Thank you," I said twisting the cap off and taking a few gulps.

"Are you sure you want to continue? We can schedule another appointment if you need to stop."

"No, I want to keep going. I need to get it all out," I said, setting the water bottle on the coffee table.

"All right. Go ahead when you're ready."

"A few years after this whole thing ended, I discovered George and Carol had called the police, and the police reached out to the FBI. Stewart discovered the authorities were searching for us, although I'm not certain how, and he wanted to marry Sapphira. That's why we left and ended up living out of tents in Alabama, because I guess it was legal for a man to marry a fourteen-year-old there at that time.

"Sophia, you and Eva stay away from the water unless there is an adult close by. There are alligators and poisonous snakes in that lake."

"They'll be all right, Grace. Sophia's a good girl. Besides, it's the perfect morning to go fishing," said Edgar, flashing a smile in my direction and winking at Mom, who seemed deep in thought. "What do you say to a fishing trip, girls?"

"That's boring," said Eva. "I'd rather play with my dolls."

"Sure," I said hesitantly, wondering what was wrong with Mom and why Edgar was suddenly being so nice.

"Great, let's grab the poles. Bait and tackle are with Jack and Mike. They drove down in the truck earlier. Come on, Eva, bring your dolls and play in the sand and dirt behind us."

Eva groaned, "I don't want to get all dirty."

"Eva, go with Edgar and Sophia. Sapphira and I have a lot to do today and you might like the fresh air by the lake," said Mom.

Eva followed behind us, pouting.

"Mike found the perfect spot early this morning before the sun was up. What do you think we'll catch?" asked Edgar.

"Um … fish?" I responded, a little freaked out by his enthusiasm. Edgar never talked this much.

Edgar chuckled, "Hopefully."

Arriving at the lake after a short walk, we found Mike and Jack fishing on wooden boat docks lining the shore. Nearby was a shack where people could order snacks and drinks. Near the docks were wooden picnic tables, each with a small table and grill next to it.

"What are those for?" I asked Edgar.

"The small table is for cleaning and scaling the fish, and the grill is for cooking them up. Nothing like fresh fish."

Tim played with blocks near his dad's chair. Eva sat nearby at one of the picnic tables with her dolls.

Edgar handed me a fishing pole. "Do you need help baiting your hook?"

"No thanks, I got this," I said, attaching the worm to the hook and casting my line. My birth dad had taken us to the mountains in Utah on a free fishing weekend to teach us. I'd caught on pretty quick.

Edgar nodded his approval and got his own fishing pole ready.

The water was green and calm, and we had the lake to ourselves. Except for the occasional sound effects Tim made with his blocks, the only noise was the rustle of leaves and the winding and casting of fishing lines. In the course of an hour, Jack caught two fish and I caught one.

Edgar called my fish a bluegill. I'd never seen such a round fish before. And small, too. I thought we would have to throw it back, but Edgar said we could keep it and I could have it for dinner.

"Daddy, can I go swimming?" asked Tim, climbing into Mike's lap as I put my fish in the cooler near his chair.

"No, it's too dangerous." Mike sat the boy on the ground again. "Sit there and play quietly."

Tim threw a block, and it splashed into the water. "No more blocks! I want to go swimming."

"Don't give me attitude, boy, now do as you're told."

Tim stood up and screamed. "I want to go swimming!"

"Son, stop whining before you scare all the fish away." Mike grabbed Tim's shirt and forced him to sit on the ground near his chair. "Now sit there and be quiet."

"Take him back to camp," Jack said.

Edgar glanced at Eva. "I don't think going back would be much fun. Unless Tim needs to take a nap?"

Tim bolted to his feet and ran toward camp. "No! No naps!"

"What are you doing, child?" yelled Mike, jumping up from his chair and running after him.

As Mike closed in on the boy, Tim swerved, giggling. "Catch me, Daddy!" and ran straight for the lake.

"Grab him, Edgar, he's heading your direction," Mike yelled.

Edgar tossed his fishing pole on the ground. "Keep an eye on that, Sophia," he said, getting up to help Mike.

I rested my foot on the pole so it wouldn't get dragged into the water if a fish tugged on the line.

Tim screeched when he saw Edgar joining the chase and changed direction again, giggling. "Can't catch me!"

Before Edgar could grab him, Tim ran straight off the wooden dock into the water below.

It reminded me of a cartoon where a character runs off a cliff and hangs in midair for a second, and I burst out laughing. Forgetting Edgar's pole, I walked closer to the edge of the dock to see what was happening. Tim flailed in the water, screaming.

Mike jumped into the water, wrapped his arm around Tim's waist, and tried to calm him down.

I shook my head and sat down to reel in mine and Edgar's line. Scanning the water for any signs of rings or bubbles that might show the fish were still around, I saw something black bobbing in the water.

"What is that?" I yelled, pointing.

Edgar looked to where I pointed. "Water moccasin headed this way," he said tensely to Mike.

"Alligator!" screamed Eva.

I looked back at her. She was pointing to the water, so I scanned the area for the large reptile. There, near the opposite bank, I spotted the alligator, swimming. Headed in our direction, probably curious about all the noise.

"Eva, get in the truck. Sophia, carry all the chairs and poles to the truck," yelled Jack.

Mike still couldn't get Tim to calm down, but managed to pull himself and Tim out of the water before either of the dangerous animals could reach them.

Jack and I tossed the fishing supplies into the back of the truck. Eva was already there, jumping up and down yelling, "Hurry up!" repeatedly.

I climbed in the back, and a moment later, Mike lifted the sopping-wet Tim into the back, too, before climbing into the cab with Edgar and Jack.

The alligator reached the shore just as we pulled away.

"That was crazy, huh kids?" yelled Edgar through the back window. "Each of you did a great job showing how our community is supposed to work. Helping each other, despite how scary things get. I'm so proud, I'm going to treat you to some fast food."

Eva and I grinned at each other. "I want chicken nuggets," yelled Eva.

I glanced at Tim, who also smiled through chattering teeth, then at Edgar, who was looking back at me. I gave him a small smile but wondered why we were being allowed to eat food that went against the community rules. *I wonder what Hannah would say if she were here.*

Jack ordered the food, and we sat in the parking lot to eat. The men set the tailgate down and joined us. I opened my kid's meal, took out the hamburger with extra pickles and ate. Eva grabbed the toy and had to be reminded twice to eat her food instead of playing with the little doll she got as a prize.

No one said much, and that gave me time to think. I felt there had to be a reason Edgar was being so nice lately, and I wanted to see how far I could push the limits with him. My eyes fixed on a gun hanging in the back window of the truck.

"Hey Edgar, what kind of gun is that?"

"It's a Remington .257 bolt-action hunting rifle."

"What does that mean? What can you hunt with it?"

"Anything you want," said Edgar, around a mouthful of food.

"Will you teach me how to hunt?" I asked.

"Yeah, sure, one of these days."

"Can I hold it?"

"Not today, kiddo."

I thought for a moment, then asked, "When you teach me, could I have a gun of my own?"

Edgar stopped chewing and examined me. A smile crept over his face. "I don't think that would be a problem, we just have to talk to your mom."

"Thank you." I smiled and finished my meal. If Edgar kept his word, I would have a way to protect myself — and my sisters.

As we got close to the campsite, Edgar poked his head out the back window again. "Girls, when we get back, go straight to your mother. We're celebrating something special today and you must get ready."

Jack pulled up behind the hotel's fenced-in swimming pool and parked.

"Daddy, are we here to go swimming?" asked Tim, when his dad climbed out of the truck.

Mike rolled his eyes. "No son, I think we've had enough swimming for today."

Eva hopped down from the back of the truck and ran toward the tent. I took my time, lingering, hoping to figure out what they were hiding from us.

Edgar reached into the bed and picked up some fishing supplies. "Sophia, help me carry some of this stuff back to camp. You can tell me what you're thinking so hard about on the way."

I took the tackle box he handed me and walked beside him. Choosing to keep the conversation on guns and not what really bothered me, I said, "Do you think Mom will let you teach me how to shoot?"

"Don't you worry about that. My job in the community is all about our security. Your mother trusts me. Now, set that gear down here and run along to get ready for the big celebration."

Inside the tent, Eva was already in a dress, twirling around and pretending to be a princess.

"There you are," Mom snapped. "Hurry and change."

A dress lay on a rolled-up sleeping bag, and I curled my lip at the sight of it. It was pink, my least favorite color, with white lace bordering the collar and sleeves. A big bow covered the middle on the front. I hated dresses.

"Wipe that disgusted look off your face and get dressed."

I knew better than to argue, so I put on the hideous dress and hoped I wouldn't have to wear it for too long. The lace made my neck itch.

"Grace, everything is ready and about to begin," said Edgar.

"Here." Mom handed me and Eva two baskets filled with rose petals. "Take these and go find Becky. She'll tell you where to go and what to do."

A knot began to form in my stomach. The only time I'd ever seen a basket full of flower petals was at a wedding. Maybe they had a weird new holiday that involved petals, because I couldn't think of anyone in the community who would be getting married. But I hadn't forgotten the conversation I'd overheard at the trailers, and the closer we got to Becky, the more my stomach knotted up.

"Hurry, girls, we're keeping the happy couple waiting," Becky said.

Wildflowers adorned chairs set up in rows facing an arch made of pine boughs. "When I tell you, you'll both walk down the middle of the chairs and sprinkle the flower petals along the path. Then you will take a seat on the front row."

So it was a wedding. Anger welled up inside me because there was nothing I could do to stop it. Surely Mom wouldn't let this happen. That's why she needed to think. Why she's been upset all day. They're forcing Sapphira into this, and maybe Mom, too.

Somewhere nearby, the wedding march began playing on a tape deck and Becky pushed us toward the aisle. "Go ahead, girls," she whispered. "Remember to sprinkle the flowers and smile."

I don't know what I did with the flowers, but I'm guessing I did what they asked, because no one yelled at me. Taking my seat, I stared at Stewart's back. He stood completely still, facing the arch. Someone tugged on the shoulder of my dress and told me to stand. I obeyed and turned. Until Edgar and Sapphira passed by, I didn't understand what was happening. Their close presence jolted me from the dreamlike state I'd been in. Sapphira wore a simple, white, long-sleeved dress that went down to her ankles. Her long hair was pulled into a braid that reached down to the middle of her back, and she held onto Edgar's arm.

Her skin was pale and her eyes looked vacant, reminding me of a movie I saw once, where a ghost had taken over a person's body and you could tell the person was no longer inside.

Sapphira reached the front, where Richard met her. "Who gives this woman to be wed?" asked Richard.

"I, Edgar, with the consent of her mother, give this woman to Stewart."

Woman? What are they talking about? She's only fourteen! I wanted to scream, but my mouth was dry and I couldn't make the sound come out.

Richard led her the few remaining feet to Stewart, who never once looked back at her. But now, he turned to her, and held her hands.

Richard proceeded with the ceremony, but skipped the part about the vows. When it was time to exchange rings, Stewart put Sapphira's ring on her, then put on his own. My sister stood up there, frozen, with a fake grin on her face. Something was very wrong. What had they done to her?

"Now that you're marrying our most holy leader, you get to choose your new, holy name," said Richard.

Sapphira blinked a few times, then, in a low voice, said, "Jasmine." Speaking seemed to snap her out of the daze she'd been in, and her eyes filled with tears.

"Do you, Jasmine Sapphira, take his holiness Stewart Warden to be your celestial husband to honor till death do you part?"

A tear rolled down my sister's cheek, but she said nothing. After a minute or two had passed, Mom stood up. "She does, under my authority," she said through gritted teeth.

I stared at Mom. What had happened to her? I was losing my family one by one. They were becoming strangers — people who looked familiar but were no longer the people I once knew. When Edgar showed us to our tent, I would pull out my notebook from its hiding place in my sleeping bag and remind myself who I was. Every day if I had to, I promised myself, and I'd remind Eva, too.

"You are now Mrs. Jasmine Sapphira Warden, and by the authority vested in me by our most holy leader, Stewart Warden, I pronounce you husband and wife," said Richard.

Stewart leaned over and kissed Sapphira. I thought I would puke. He wiped away her tears, and as I was near them, I heard him whisper, "I hope those are tears of joy, my love. This will all be over soon."

I knew they weren't tears of joy, and something about the way he said those words made me think he knew they weren't, either. Was Sapphira's life in danger? I needed to convince Edgar to teach me how to shoot that gun as soon as possible.

Chapter 11

The darkness in the tent slowly lightened as the sun came up. I stared at the wall of our tent as the questions that had plagued me all night continued rolling through my brain. What bothered me most was not being sure if Mom had really agreed to let Sapphira marry Stewart, or if they had forced her. Would Edgar continue being nice, or was he simply the distraction? What had happened to Sapphira after the wedding, and would I see her today?

As soon as it was light enough, I pulled my notebook out of its hiding place and wrote down the questions, hoping it would help me clear my head. Slow, shuffling footsteps sounded outside. My heart raced, and I jammed the notebook back into my sleeping bag and listened. The footsteps stopped just outside.

A moment later I heard a tent zipper open, then shuffling and stomping noises, then the zipper again. Somebody coughed, then swore.

"Sam." It was Edgar's voice. He spoke a little above a whisper. "Sam, quick, run to the hotel and call animal control."

Something hissed near the entrance of our tent, and I jumped. Edgar swore again.

"Edgar, what's going on?" I asked.

"Be quiet and stay in your tent. There's an alligator out here."

The sounds of everyone waking up and getting ready for the day increased, and I heard Edgar warning people about the alligator.

Curiosity got the best of me, and I moved to the entrance of the tent and opened the zipper just enough to peek through. Green scaly skin met my eyes. It was so close I could have stuck my fingers out and touched it.

"They're on their way," Sam said, in a breathy voice. He must have been running. "Should we try to lure it away?"

"Might be dangerous." Richard's voice.

"That guy is at least twelve feet long. The best thing to do is leave it be. We don't want it to feel more threatened than it already does," said Edgar.

As if on cue, the alligator made a deep, growling noise. I jumped and scrambled toward the back of the tent.

Eva sat up, wide-eyed. "What was that?"

I shushed her and motioned for her to sit next to me. She obeyed, and I wrapped my arms around her.

The animal outside hissed again.

"What *is* that?" whispered Eva.

"Alligator. Want to see it?"

Eva wrapped her arms around me and buried her face in my shoulder. "No, I don't want to get eaten by an alligator."

"Animal control is here," I heard Sam say.

"I've told the hotel they can't let people camp here. The alligators love this spot. You might consider a new location after we get this big guy out of here," said a new voice I didn't recognize.

"Yeah, this is our second run-in. We'll definitely be moving as soon as possible," Edgar replied.

"All right, when my partner and I get these nooses around his neck, he'll probably flip a few times, so everyone stand back. We'll be able to drag him a safe distance away from the tents and tie him up over there."

As the animal control person spoke, I crawled toward the front of the tent and moved the zipper up a few inches.

"Don't leave," cried Eva.

"Shh, I'm not leaving, I just want to get a better look."

I peeked out of the hole I'd made. The green scaly skin met my eyes, less than six inches away. It twitched a little, then the animal hissed again. I jumped, struggled to zip the flap closed, and scrambled to the back of the tent.

"How close is it?" whispered Eva.

I put her hand on my chest so she could feel my rapid heartbeat. "Close."

For a minute or two nothing happened, then someone grunted. It was light enough now that I could see shadows outside. The alligator thrashed, and our tent shook.

Eva screamed and wouldn't stop, even after I covered her mouth with my hand.

"Watch that tail!" someone yelled.

"Nooses are on. Toss me that rope."

The thrashing continued for a minute or two longer, then stopped. It sounded like they were dragging the alligator away. Eva's screams were replaced by sobs.

"Okay, toss the jacket over his eyes. Let's get him in the truck. You two grab his legs on that side; we'll take the legs on this side," said the unfamiliar voice.

More sounds of struggling, a loud thump, and then the tailgate of a truck being closed. A moment later, the door of our tent opened and Mom's face appeared.

"You can come out now girls," Edgar said nearby.

"My babies. Oh, I was so scared when I saw that alligator. Are you okay?"

I hugged Mom and looked over at the animal control truck to see how big the alligator was. Its tail was sticking out of the back of the truck a good five feet. On the side of the truck I read, *Animal Control of Alabama*. I hadn't realized we'd gone to a new state when we left the farm.

"My flock!" Stewart walked up to us, a big, creepy grin on his face and his arms stretched out. He seemed unaware of the close encounter we'd all just had. "Today is a day of rejoicing! The Lord has shown me a vision. My new bride, Jasmine, is to be kept apart for a full twenty-four hours. She will join us for a special celebration feast this evening. The Lord is shining his face on our community and has promised Jasmine and I a son if we obey this command.

"Richard, Jack, I need you to go find a new place for us to plant our community. This place is not safe for children, so I expect you back this evening. The children will do no work today. It is their day of rest.

"We will assist with the installation of several bathtubs in the hotel. The children have two rules: Stay clear of the bathtubs and the lake. We can't have the future generations of our community hurt."

Stewart's eyes were wide as he spoke, and his blond hair stuck out from his head. He looked even crazier when he was happy. But where was Sapphira? I could check on her while everyone was distracted.

Hannah appeared with Lindsey. I waved, but she didn't wave back. She looked upset. I walked over and told her about our free day.

"I know. I wanted to stay in the hotel, but Dad said I had to come outside and play with you guys," said Hannah.

"Did you hear about the alligator?" Eva asked.

Hannah nodded. "That must have been scary."

"It was. What should we do today?" asked Eva.

Hannah shrugged.

"What's wrong, Hannah?" I asked.

"My grandparents are coming today, and they're taking me and my mom away to live with them."

"Why are they taking you away? Are you coming back?" asked Eva.

"Mom says I'll never see Dad again if she can help it," said Hannah. "She's mad he married your sister. Especially since she's only three years older than me, and there are other men who could take care of her."

I was mad, too, but I couldn't tell Hannah that. "I'll miss hanging out with you," I said. "But I'm glad you get to see your grandparents. I wish I could see my family again."

"I don't want to live with my grandparents. They don't understand why we need this community. Um … is Eva supposed to be doing that?" Hannah pointed behind me.

I glanced over my shoulder and spotted Eva climbing into a bathtub.

"Eva, get out of there!" I yelled, running to her and looking to see if any adults had noticed her.

"What? I'm pretending it's my ship."

"Didn't you hear Stewart? He told us not to go near the bathtubs."

Eva climbed out. I grabbed her arm and pulled her back to where Hannah stood. "Let's play a game before Eva gets us all in trouble."

We spent the rest of the morning and afternoon playing with my trucks and Eva's dolls.

Becky returned to camp before the others to work on the feast Stewart had talked about. "Want to help me cook tonight, girls?" she asked.

"I can't," said Hannah. "Mom wants me back at the hotel." She waved at me and Eva and headed off.

"I'll help," said Eva.

"Me, too," I said.

"Great, Eva, you can shuck corn, and Sophia, you can cut the other vegetables."

Not long after we'd started our tasks, Edgar showed up. "Becky, I hate to take your help away, but I need to talk to the girls for a minute. Sophia, Eva, please come here."

We obeyed, following him to where the bathtubs were laid out.

"One bathtub we installed had to be cleaned again. It looked like someone had been standing in it with dirty shoes." Edgar looked down at our feet, his eyebrows raised. "When I saw Hannah returning to the hotel, I asked if she knew anything, and she said Eva was playing in it. Is that true?"

Eva hung her head. "I forgot Stewart told us not to."

"And where were you, Sophia?"

"I was close. Hannah and I were talking, and I didn't notice Eva wander off, but I made her get out when I saw her."

"Eva, I'm going to make sure you don't forget the rules ever again. Sophia, take your sister down to the trees at the back of the hotel and help her cut a switch, then bring it back. Be quick, I have things to do before dinner."

I nodded and grabbed Eva's hand. We walked fast, and I tried to think even faster. If I tried to hide her, they would come looking for us and punish us both. Part of me wished I could leave with Hannah and Lindsey.

We passed the row of bathrooms where Mom took us to take showers and made us wear flip-flops because of poisonous tree frogs, and I got an idea. Opening the door to one, I pushed Eva inside.

"What are you doing?" she asked.

"Pull your pants down so I can pad your butt with toilet paper."

"Why?"

"Because Edgar's going to whip you and it will hurt, that's why," I said, undoing the button on her jeans.

Eva pulled her pants down, and I stuffed toilet paper into her underwear. When I finished, I had her pull her pants up again, then adjusted the paper so it looked more natural.

"All right, now, when he hits you, cry. Pinch yourself really hard or something. He has to believe your tears are real."

Eva nodded. We reached the trees Edgar told us about, and I broke one off and handed it to my little sister. "Let's get this over with."

Back at camp, Edgar waited for us. He held out his hand and Eva gave him the switch.

"Come here and bend over my knee," he said.

Eva obeyed.

I stood nearby chewing my nails, hoping my plan would work.

Edgar wacked it against Eva's behind four or five times. Eva cried out after each swat, and when she stood up, her face was wet with tears.

"Next time, I hope you won't forget the rules," said Edgar, tossing the switch into a fire pit as he headed back toward the hotel. "You can have your helpers back now, Becky."

"I'll be right back. I'm going to help Eva wash her face," I told Becky. I took her into our tent, helped her pull the toilet paper out of her pants, then used some of it to wipe her face. "Did it hurt?" I asked.

"Not really, but it was scary."

"Don't worry, we'll tell Mom and she'll take care of it," I said.

We headed out of the tent, and saw Mom returning to camp. As we told her what happened, Stewart came out of his trailer and started yelling for everyone to gather around the feast for a special meeting. Eva and I went back out to help Becky after we told Mom, only to find that she had already finished everything she had asked us to help her with while we were gone, and the table was set up nicely. The glasses were to the right of each plate, with the knife blades facing the plates on top of perfectly folded napkins.

"My dear family, we are taking this evening to celebrate the holy union between me and my beautiful new bride, Jasmine. We have obeyed the Lord's command, and I expect we'll be seeing signs of the son he's promised very soon."

Everyone clapped, and Stewart held his hand out to Sapphira, who took it. They walked to the table together. My sister wore a shy grin and kept her eyes on the ground. When they reached the table, Sapphira sat on Stewart's left. The chair next to her was open, so I took it quickly before anyone could tell me no.

"Sophia, that spot is for Lindsey," said Becky. "Wives must sit to the left of their husbands to show submission and bring them tranquility. We were created out of man, so when we marry, we belong to our husbands. And it shows who each woman belongs to, so other men won't lust after them. Why don't you take a seat farther down the table?"

"But I thought Lindsey and Hannah left." I glanced around the table.

Stewart glared at me.

"Edgar, what is this I hear about you spanking Eva?" Mom yelled across the clearing as she came out of the tent Eva and I slept in.

Edgar, who had taken a seat across from Stewart, turned in his chair to face Mom as she stomped up to him.

"Eva disobeyed the rules, so as her father, I punished her," said Edgar.

"I am the only one allowed to punish my kids. If they need correction, you tell me and I will take care of it," Mom shouted shaking a finger in his face.

"GRACE!" shouted Stewart, rising to his feet. "You forget your place. Submit to your husband. Edgar is in charge of your family, and I am in charge of this community. You should hang your head in shame at your sinful outburst."

"No, you forget your place. These are my kids and I can take them out of this community. You don't control me!" Mom shouted.

A slow, creepy grin spread over Stewart's face. "Is that so?" He jerked Sapphira's arm. "Stand up."

Sapphira obeyed, and Stewart led her back toward the trailer.

Chapter 12

Mom's jaw moved back and forth as we watched Stewart walk off with my older sister. Everyone around the table stared at Mom with shocked expressions. I hated that Sapphira was stuck with Stewart, but Mom yelling at him impressed me, and it was hard to keep a prideful grin from my face.

Beep, beep.

A big yellow bus rolled into the camp and stopped. Richard and Jack climbed out and greeted everyone with a big smile. "We found our next temporary home," said Jack. He looked around, and the smile faded. "Did I miss something?"

No one answered him.

By now Sapphira had entered the trailer, and Stewart locked the door behind her before returning to join the men standing near the front bumper of the bus.

"Family, come see our new home on wheels. This is perfect, guys, good job on listening to God," Stewart said.

"You expect us all to live in this thing?" asked Sam.

"Well, not all of us. There's a house we might get, but we're waiting for Edgar's militia contact to get back to us. We can split the group up for a while; families with children will live in the bus. Jack, Sam, and Richard will stay here and continue working at the hotel and painting billboards. Those on the bus will help Edgar deliver the military supplies to our militia friends. What do you think, Mike?"

"It won't be comfortable with three kids and six adults. What do you suppose we do to accommodate?" asked Mike.

"The benches can be taken out or rearranged and used as beds. We can cut a hole through the floor in the back for a toilet, and set the front up as a mini kitchen with a table bolted to the floor and take some of the benches and place them at the table for eating areas. We have plenty of them to do with what we want. "

"Sounds well thought out," said Stewart. "Let's take a look."

After the feast, which was eaten quickly and in silence, the men climbed inside, talked, and measured things.

The following day, we started the remodel. Living in a bus sounded like fun at first, but by the end of the remodel, I was sick of looking at the big, ugly yellow turd.

The three single men stayed in camp instead of going to the hotel. They tore seats out of the bus and nominated Eva and me to carry trash to the dumpster behind the hotel, which wasn't very far since they parked right by it. We also fetched tools and water for them. We were basically their slaves for two days while they figured things out.

On day three, they finished throwing junk out of the stupid bus and spent the rest of the day fishing and setting up a telescope. Apparently there was going to be a meteor shower over the next few days. We were instructed not to touch it.

One more armload of trash for each of us and we were done, thank God! I updated Becky on the progress and told her we were going to play.

"Wait, girls. Before you go, I need your help."

Becky's arms were full of old sheets and towels when we reached her.

"Good ol' Yellow," I said, patting the side.

Everyone chuckled at the name.

"I like that name," said Eva.

"All right, girls, we need to make curtains and a nice privacy wall for our rustic bathroom back here." She walked to the back of the bus, stared at the hole in the floor and shook her head.

"That's supposed to be our bathroom?" asked Eva.

"Yes," Becky sighed. "May God grant us a place for our community to put roots down soon."

"Amen," said Eva.

I wanted to tell Eva to stop saying "amen" to their stupid prayers, but I knew it was best, for her sake, not to mention it.

Becky pulled out a hammer and some nails from a bag sitting on one of the benches. "Sophia, I need you to stand on the bench and hold the towel in place over the window as I hammer in the nails to keep it up. Eva, I need you to hand me nails as I ask for them."

Once we were done with the windows, it was on to the rustic bathroom. When the sheet didn't work, Becky pulled out a big blue tarp. Once we finally got it nailed in place, she added a few more nails for good measure.

"This should work."

"Yeah, that'll be way better than sheets. No one will see through," said Eva.

"Thanks for your help, girls, why don't you check out the rest of the bus while I finish up a few things?"

There were four beds total, which meant we'd be sharing. I watched Becky go around and add a few more nails to each towel to make sure they didn't come off the windows.

"Eva, why don't you go get all your things and bring them into the bus—except your sleeping bags and pillows, which you'll need for tonight," Becky said. "Sophia, there is one more thing we need before you go get your things. Will you please run over to where we keep the painting supplies and grab one of the empty white buckets?"

I got the requested item and Becky sawed off the bottom. "The men may be fine using a hole in the floor, but us girls need to sit on something."

When she finished, she put the cut side into the hole. "There, we'll have the men figure out how to glue that in so it's safe to sit on. Then we'll send the men to find a toilet seat for the top."

I didn't mind Becky; she was nice to us, a good mom to Tim, and she was the best cook in the community. When she was in charge of us, I knew we wouldn't get yelled at.

Once we were done turning the bus into a house, we were sent off to play. I ran toward Sapphira's trailer, to where Jack, Richard, Edgar, and Mike were huddled around the telescope they'd set up.

"You saw it, Edgar, didn't you?" asked Jack, as I walked up.

"Yeah, it was zigzagging across the sky. Definitely not a meteor or plane."

"I think you're all pulling my chain," said Mike.

"Now, Mike, you know I don't pull anyone's chain, and I'm telling you, there was a UFO flying around up there while you were looking through the scope," Richard said.

Mike scratched the back of his head and stared up at the sky.

"What are you boys doing?" asked Mom, walking up to them.

"There is something zigzagging in the sky, do you see it?" asked Edgar.

I looked up and saw what they were talking about. Fascinated by the small object zigzagging through the clouds, I wondered if there was an alien force watching us. While they were preoccupied, I walked up to the telescope and tried to look through the lens.

"Hey, get your filthy hands off that. Telescope is for adult use only," barked Richard.

I jumped and stepped back, then looked at Edgar.

"Sorry, kiddo, rules are rules."

Later that evening, I, Eva, and Tim decided we really wanted to look through the scope. We knew we weren't to touch it, but we thought we could look through the lens without actually making contact.

Of course, we were caught red-handed. "What did we tell you about touching the telescope?" Richard yelled.

Sam and Mike followed closely behind him, and each man grabbed a kid and carried us into Sapphira and Stewart's trailer.

They stuffed socks into our mouths, taped them in place, then swatted us in turn with the paddle.

I could barely breathe with the sock in my mouth, and crying made it even harder. I looked at Eva, whose face was pale and wet with tears. Furious, I elbowed Richard in the face and was able to get free. I took the sock out of my mouth and screamed at the top of my lungs for Mom as I ran to Eva, and ripped the sock from her mouth as well.

Suddenly, Mom threw open the trailer door and took Eva up in her arms. "What the hell did I tell you about touching my girls? The next time you try anything like this, you will never see us again. Do you understand?"

The next day we took down camp and were on the road. I didn't really want to leave this place, but I was excited to travel around in Ol' Yellow. We drove all day, only stopping so Stewart could trade places with Mike or Edgar at the wheel. A few hours after we started out, I made my way to the front, where Mom was chatting with Becky.

"Mom," I whispered in her ear, "I have to go to the bathroom. Can you ask Stewart when we're stopping?"

"We don't need to stop," Mom said, "just go." She didn't bother whispering.

Sapphira, Edgar, and Becky stared at me, and my face grew hot. "But I have to poop," I whispered through gritted teeth. It was becoming an emergency now.

"That doesn't matter. A toilet is a toilet even if it's moving," said Edgar.

"The bucket is secure, if that's what you're worried about," said Becky.

Again, heat filled my cheeks. "But that's gross! What if my poo flies onto another car?"

Everyone except Stewart laughed.

"The bus isn't stopping, so get in there and go. This talk is sinful," said Stewart.

I walked to the back of the bus and did my business, expecting to hear squealing tires and crushing metal as my poop smeared across someone's windshield. I hoped it wouldn't blind them. But then, imagining the scene, I giggled; I guess it was kind of funny.

No sounds of a fiery crash came, and when I finished, I curled up in a ball on my bed with Wooby. I had thought I would be embarrassed, but the more I thought about it, the funnier it was. Finding humor in every situation always made things easier.

Someone cleared their throat above me, and I twisted on the bed to see who it was. Stewart stared down at me. "Sin causes shame. I hope you remember this and learn from it."

I buried my face in my blanket. I truly hated him. All these rules, and no one ever told us what they were until we broke them. It wasn't fair.

Eva and I shared one bed. It was cramped, but not as bad as for the adults. Mike, Becky and Tim shared one, Mom and Edgar shared the third, and the fourth was for Stewart and Sapphira. I felt sick to my stomach any time I saw my older sister with him, and I wished there was something I could do to help her.

During our time on Ol' Yellow, we traveled through several states, sometimes staying in campgrounds, sometimes in the parking lot of a grocery store or other place of business.

One campsite we stayed at had pit toilets. Mom took us there in the evening to wash ourselves with baby wipes.

"Watch out for snakes and frogs. Many of them are poisonous and could kill us," she said.

Eva grabbed my arm and whimpered.

"See my footprints in the mud?" I said.

She nodded.

"Step in my footprints. You search the ground on this side, and I'll look on this side, okay?"

"Okay." She released her grip on my arm but held onto the back of my shirt.

Once at the bathroom, we cleaned up, then returned to the bus without seeing a single deadly frog or snake.

"Everyone load up. We'll be driving all night," said Stewart, who sat behind the wheel. "Before we get too far, I would like all three children to come forward so I can explain some things to them."

Great, another night of Stewart talking to himself. That guy is seriously crazy.

"Things are going to start changing around here," said Stewart, looking at us from the big mirror at the front of the bus. "During prayer, you young ones will keep your hands raised. It's important to raise our hands when we pray. The air above our heads becomes charged with our words. It's the meeting ground between us and heaven, and raising our hands makes the power stay here. If we don't, it moves around like a cloud. So you need to practice keeping your hands up."

We didn't respond, and he finally left us alone and talked to himself the rest of the night.

Chapter 13

Every few days we would stop and park in various parking lots. Edgar and the others would take giant duffel bags out of locked containers at the front of the bus and leave for the day. When they returned, the bags would be empty. At the next place we stopped, the empty bags would come back full. Eva, Tim, and I were never allowed to see what was inside the bags.

We were not allowed to leave the bus while the adults were gone, and it was hard entertaining ourselves in such a cramped space. A week into our bus adventure, we were all pretty grumpy. Tim was the worst. At four years old, he had a lot of energy, and being cooped up on the bus made him angry. When the adults left for the day, he would cry and complain about everything, which annoyed me and Eva. After three days of trying to console him, I'd had enough.

We were parked at a shopping mall next to a high school with a large field behind it.

"Eva," I said, "I'm going to take Tim over to the field at the school so he can get some energy out. I'm sick of him crying and throwing tantrums all day long."

"I want to go," said Eva.

"Are you sure? We might get in trouble."

"I don't care, I HAVE to get out of this stupid bus!" Eva said dramatically.

"Okay, let's go."

Tim rode on my back until we got to the grass, where I set him down. He immediately ran off, so to make sure he didn't run too far away from us, we started a game of tag.

We played until we couldn't run anymore, then lay down on the grass to rest. A bell inside the school rang and kids poured out of the building.

"We better get back, it's getting late." I said.

They agreed, but when we told Tim it was time to leave, he cried again.

"It'll be okay. We can get something to eat when we get back. Aren't you hungry?" I asked.

He shook his head, kicked his legs on the ground, and let out a piercing scream. I glanced toward the kids coming out of the school and hoped they would ignore us.

"We'll have to leave him here by himself if he keeps kicking like that," I said.

"We could drag him," said Eva, not understanding that I didn't really mean to leave him.

"NO," screamed Tim, and he scrambled to his feet and folded his arms, "No dragging."

I smiled. "Are you going to come with us now?"

He nodded and reached for my hand, and the three of us headed back.

When the bus came into sight we slowed. The adults were back. What could I tell them that wouldn't get us in trouble? If Tim would be a good, happy boy, I could tell them he needed to get energy out. He was doing fine now, but would he stay that way?

Mike stood outside waiting for us. Tim ran to his dad, telling him: "We got to play tag, and I won sometimes."

Mike knelt next to his son. "That's great, son. I need you to go inside now."

Tim obeyed.

"We told you to stay on the bus. Your mother has been worried sick," said Mike.

"Sorry," muttered Eva.

I wasn't sorry, I wanted to explain that it was something we needed to do, but he didn't care. None of them did.

"Sophia, do you have anything to say?"

I looked him in the eyes. "Tim wouldn't stop crying, so I took him to the grassy area over there so he could run around for a while, and it worked."

Mike didn't say anything but pointed to the door and waited for us to march past before getting on the bus himself.

That evening, Stewart lectured us on our sinful ways, and I thought that was the end of it.

For the next two days, Tim constantly asked to go outside again and when he was told no, he cried and wouldn't stop. His parents did everything they could to get him to calm down, and so did we, but nothing worked.

On the last day, Tim clung to his mom and refused to let go until Becky agreed to stay behind. He finally stopped crying for a few minutes. I was so happy I could have danced, but I could tell the adults weren't pleased to be losing one of their workers.

By the time the others returned, everyone was exhausted. Tim had fallen asleep twenty minutes before the adults came back, and the moment they entered, he woke up and cried again.

"Shut him up," yelled Mike after ten minutes of constant screaming.

"He's been doing this all day," said Becky. "I don't know what's wrong, and I'm afraid he's going to make himself sick."

"I do. If the girls hadn't taken him outside, he would be fine," said Mike, pacing up and down the aisle.

I sat on the edge of my bed, across from where Becky sat holding Tim, in case she needed me to get her anything. *If only I could take them back in time and show them how Tim had been crying for days before now.* Becky laid Tim down on the bed and covered him with a blanket. He fought her and sat up, his sobs turning into screams.

"That's it. This has gone on too long." Mike grabbed Tim from Becky's arms, stuffed a sock into his mouth and taped it there. Then he tied the boy's hands behind his back and put him face-down on the floor.

Before I knew what was happening, I found myself in the same position. The sock tasted of salt and dirt, smelled like rotten eggs, and I started gagging. I tried to free my hands, but the more I struggled, the more the rope cut into my wrists. From the noises behind me I could tell that Eva was getting the same treatment.

"This will teach you girls to disobey," said Mike.

Next to me I heard the *thwack, thwack,* of a paddle and Tim's muted screams. My heart raced and I squeezed my eyes closed. A moment later I felt the sting of the paddle and cried out, but that caused the sock to go farther back in my mouth and made it difficult to breathe.

I wasn't aware of anything for the next several minutes, except struggling to get air into my lungs. Ages passed before someone tore the tape from my mouth and I was able to spit out the disgusting sock.

"Where is my mom?" I screamed.

I lay on the floor of the bus for several minutes, gasping for air, before attempting to stand. When I got to my feet, my eyes sought Mom. She had said she wouldn't let this happen again. But Mom sat at the front, staring blankly at the floor, seeming lost in her own little world. I wasn't even sure she was hearing Tim's screams.

"Why don't we stop there for today and schedule another appointment?" Stacy suggested.

"Sure, I didn't think telling my story would use up so much of my energy, but I'm exhausted."

Stacy smiled. "I can imagine. When we experience traumatic events, that trauma affects our whole body. In telling your story, you're actually reliving those painful moments as if they're happening to you all over again. I'm starting to understand better why you wouldn't want to trust any religion, or religious leader.

There were a lot of normal childhood experiences that were twisted. At some point, I would love to pray through those traumatic memories with you so you can be healed of them."

A normal therapist probably would have said they wanted to help me process the memories so they wouldn't be so traumatic. I wasn't so sure about adding God into the mix, but Stacy seemed genuine in her sympathy and concern. "I never considered that my past was still affecting me, but that makes sense," I replied. "It would be nice to be free of all this."

"Well, we can talk more about that at a later date. First, I want you to finish telling me your story so we can build a trusting relationship. This week, if you feel comfortable, I want to you to try praying whenever those memories surface. Simply ask God to bring you comfort and help you process those memories in a healthy way. I think it will help."

"Sure, if you think it will help, I'll try it."

"When would you like to meet again?" asked Stacy.

We set a time for the following week and I left, feeling tired but somehow a little lighter, too.

Chapter 14

"How have you been doing since our meeting last week?" Stacy asked.

"I've been reliving memories, and I feel like I'm lashing out at people more. Like I've been feeling irrationally angry. But I have been trying to pray like you suggested."

"Would it be okay if we pray before we start today?" asked Stacy.

"Sure," I said, curious to see if her prayers would be any different from the ones I heard growing up.

"Lord thank you that your love is healing and that you're always with us. Father, I ask that you please help Sophia clearly remember as she continues her story. And help her to heal from this as she talks about it. Please guide our conversation and protect Sophia as she relives these memories."

The casual nature of it surprised me and brought me comfort.

"Are you ready to begin?" asked Stacy.

"I am."

7 Months Before The FBI Standoff

The sun was setting when we parked the bus for the night. A deep, pulsing sound reached my ears, and I sat up in my bed. A neon cowboy with the name Buckaroo Ale House under it blinked on and off on top of a small building. It was time for the empty duffel bags to be refilled.

My bed at the back of the bus had become my safe haven, the only place I could go to be alone. At least, as alone as a person could be on a crowded bus. I deeply felt the injustice of the paddling we had all received and wanted as much distance between myself and them as possible.

Whatever was happening with Mom scared me, and I watched her from my spot. She'd been normal for the past day and a half. I wanted to tell her what they'd done to us, but she'd been there. Was it possible for someone to be so totally unaware in that kind of situation? I found it hard to believe, but remembering her empty gaze made me doubt myself.

Stewart stood in the aisle and cleared his throat. Everyone turned their attention to him. "Alcohol is a sin. I know several of those in our community have struggled with this addiction in the past. Tonight will be a true test to see if they can resist temptation. Since our children have proved they cannot resist temptation, they need us to be the example."

When he finished preaching, Edgar and Mike headed inside the bar with two of the large duffel bags.

"All right, girls, it's time for bed," said Mom.

I turned away from her and stared out the window.

"Baby, what's wrong?" she asked, sitting on the bed next to me and rubbing my back.

A disgusted huff escaped me. I couldn't take it anymore. "Why did you let Mike hit us like that? You promised you wouldn't let it happen, but you just sat there!" I said, trying to keep my voice low.

Mom cocked her head to one side. "What are you talking about?"

BANG, BANG, BANG.

"Everyone on the floor," yelled Becky.

I covered my head with my arms and flattened myself on the bed. Eva screamed.

BANG, BANG.

Tim and Eva started to cry. The sounds of gunfire erupted and filled the night air.

"Get on the floor, girls," Mom shouted.

Soon, everyone except Stewart was crouched on the floor between the beds. The sounds got louder and louder. One ... two ... three ... I counted each time the bus shuddered. Under the loud booms of the guns was a smaller *ting, ting, ting*, as bullets hit the side of our bus.

Everyone was either screaming or sobbing, and outside it sounded like a stampede of horses.

"Sophia!" Stewart shouted my name from the front of the bus.

Lifting my head from the ground, I looked at Stewart, who was still sitting in the driver's seat as though it were a normal evening.

"Come up here next to me," he shouted over the noise.

I shook my head, my heart pounding so hard I thought it would break out of my chest.

"Don't force me to drag you."

"Please, Stewart, don't make her do this, it's not safe," sobbed Mom.

"Sophia, God has sent you a test tonight. Come up here."

He's crazy, he's insane, I won't do it. I can't. Tears flooded my eyes and my whole body trembled.

BANG, BANG.

The bus shuddered again. Four.

"The waves of a stormy sea distracted Peter during his test of faith. You are letting the noise of men fighting distract you. I won't stand for it. GET UP!"

"Go, Sophia, before he comes and gets you." Mom wrapped her arm around me. "Crawl on the floor, don't stand up."

Wiping my arm across my eyes and nose, I looked at Stewart again. His eyes were wide and evil. Mom was right. If I didn't go, Stewart might do something worse.

I lifted myself onto shaky limbs and crawled toward the front of the bus. A window shattered and pieces of glass fell on me. I stopped, frozen, and sobbing.

"Don't look at the surrounding waves. Keep your eyes on me, your savior and god, and I will keep you safe," bellowed Stewart.

I wanted to return to Mom and the others, where it felt safer. Sirens sounded in the distance. The police would make the shooting stop. Soon it would be over. I relaxed a little at the thought and, when I reached Stewart's side, I looked again into his crazy eyes.

He sat with his arms resting on his knees, glaring at me. When our eyes met, he pointed at me and then to the steps leading out of the bus. Did he want me to go outside? My breathing came in spasms, but I forced myself to crawl down the steps and huddled by the door. *Please don't open the door, I don't want to go out there.*

"Yes, bow at the feet of your savior. Who brought you out of the world and into a holy community where you can be cleansed of your sins and enter the holy, celestial body of true believers ..."

Stewart's voice trailed off and became a buzzing in the background. My mind went blank, my body numb. Suddenly I was surrounded by a bright, white light. There was a tightness around my neck as if I were choking. It was getting harder to breathe, and I felt myself slipping away to a familiar place. A soft voice was near me, but I saw no one.

"I'm here. Wake up."

I opened my eyes, still huddled on the stairs of the bus, and stared at the bolts and hardware that attached the driver's seat to the floor. My mind was empty of all thoughts but one. That white light was a familiar comfort, and I tried to cling to it. When someone finally lifted me off the floor and carried me to my bed, I barely noticed.

"Wow, okay, let's stop there for a minute and talk about this," said Stacy.

I chuckled. "That part is pretty intense."

"Uh, yeah! Are you okay? Do you need to take a break?"

"No, I'm okay," I said.

"Do you mind if I ask you some questions about this experience?"

"No, I don't mind."

"It breaks my heart, hearing you had to go through something like that, especially as a child. Do you know how long you had to stay huddled there?"

I shook my head. "It felt like hours, but I checked out."

"Do you know who spoke to you when you saw the white light? Was it someone in the group?"

"No, it's like the voice came from inside me, like it was telepathic or something. The same thing happened when I was seven."

"Hmm, I have some thoughts about that, but I think I'll wait before we talk about it. You say this has happened before? What happened when you were seven?" asked Stacy.

"I died."

"You died?" asked Stacy. "Would you be willing to tell me about that experience?

"I don't mind. There are parts I remember in great detail and some I don't remember at all. Eva, my friend Angie and I were playing Cowboys and Indians on the monkey bars." I shook my head and chuckled.

Chapter 15

"Eva, you're the Indian because we're the cowboys," I said.

"But I'm always the Indian, and you guys tie me up and hide my dolls."

"We promise we won't, right, Sophia?" said Angie.

"Yeah, I'll even let you catch me this time."

"Pinky-swear?" said Eva.

I held my hand out to my little sister; she smiled and linked her little finger with mine.

"The slide is our space," I yelled, running in that direction.

"The tribe attacks tonight, so be ready," shouted Eva.

Angie and I climbed the monkey bars to inspect the town and figure out where to put traps.

"Time out! I have to go potty," said Eva.

"I need to go, too. I'll be right back," said Angie.

While they were gone, I searched for a rope so we could escape if Eva set our buildings on fire. My stepdad had a bunch in the garage. A short rope lay on the concrete floor behind the garage door. Perfect. Back at the playground, I tried to remember what my Uncle Bill said about the quick release knot used to tie up horses.

Making the loop big enough for me to sit in, I attached the other end of the rope to the monkey bars, then climbed up to test it out.

While holding onto the bar, I scooted to the edge, put my feet through the loop and wiggled it under my behind so I would be sitting in it when I lowered myself down. I held onto the top of the rope and swung myself off the monkey bars. As soon as I dropped, my butt slipped from the rope. The loop of rope caught under my arm pits and squeezed my chest.

Oh crap, oh crap, oh crap.

If I could get one arm out, it might loosen. I forced my fingers under the rope and wiggled one arm through, then the other.

But I didn't fall to the ground as expected. Instead, the rope tightened around my throat.

"Sophia, stop. That's not funny, I know you aren't dead," Eva said, back from the bathroom and standing there with her hands on her hips.

My head throbbed and everything started to get blurry. I wanted to scream at her to run for help, but I couldn't get air to my lungs.

"I'm serious, Sophia, you're scaring me! Stop that or I'm telling mom!" Finally, Eva turned and stormed away.

Moments later, Mom ran toward me wearing only a t-shirt. I found myself wanting to laugh at the sight.

"Call 911!" she yelled to Eva.

"But mom, that's only on TV."

My vision blurred completely.

"Go get a knife, Eva; Angie, go call 911 now."

I stood beside Mom, fascinated by the sight of my hanging body. Why wasn't I afraid? My body was there, but I was here. What was happening?

A creature, maybe an angel, or a man, I'm not sure what he was, stood nearby. I looked at my mom and back at him. It was like looking through a two-way mirror, only there were no walls and nothing stopping me from touching my mom. I could see her, but she could not see me. It was as if I was in a different world, watching real life through a screen.

I knew he wanted me to go with him. He stared at me. His eyes looked like swirling flames. He was wearing a robe that was blue-green and white and sparkled with flecks of gold and silver.

His robe had silver bars along the neckline that wrapped from one shoulder to the other. Each silver bar was lined with many gold circles that from a distance seemed to float in place.

He was tall and beautiful, and every part of me wanted to wrap my arms around him. Oddly, he seemed to understand this without either of us speaking a word."

My mom continued to scream. Eva ran outside with a knife, but it was only a butter knife. Mom always put the sharp knives out of our reach.

"A butter knife!?!" Mom cried.

"What?"

Mom tried to cut the rope, but screamed, "It's not working!" and threw the knife to the ground.

The man-creature walked over, stood on the opposite side of the monkey bars, lifted his arm and made a circling motion with his finger.

Mom paused for an instant, as if she saw the rope unwinding, before trying to lift me up with one arm and trying to pull the loop away from my neck. Did she see the man too?

"Help me, please!" she yelled at the sky.

Again, the circle motion, and finally my limp body crumpled in the dirt. He had saved me, but why was I still here?

Then the scene in front of me disappeared, and I stood on clouds. Bright, white light radiated from him and surrounded us. Questions swirled in my brain. I somehow knew he had the ability to read my thoughts, but he didn't give me any answers. Instead, he pointed. I turned to look and saw a hole in the pure white light. I saw my aunt. She was on her knees in a bathroom stall with the door open. Her elbows were on the toilet lid and her hands on her face. She was crying and praying.

The hole closed. His voice sounded in my head. "You can stay, but it's better for you to return."

I wanted to stay. It was warm, loving, and like home to me, but I felt his words held more meaning. That he had bigger plans for me.

Everything inside of me wanted to please him, and before I could tell him I'd go back, he pointed at me.

A loud beeping noise woke me. My eyes fluttered open and Mom stood over me.

"Baby, you're awake." Her face was white, and tears streamed down her face. "Nurse!" she yelled, turning away from me. "She's awake!"

My body trembled like I was cold, but I didn't feel cold. People rushed toward me, shone lights in my eyes, and poked at me with weird shiny things.

"Mommy!" I screamed in a hoarse voice and tried to sit. Something pulled against my arm. A clear tube trailed from the back of my hand. "Mom!" I screamed it louder this time.

"I'm here, baby, I'm right here. Let the doctors check you. It'll be okay," Mom said, from somewhere close by.

The crowd of doctors and nurses finally released me. Mom hugged me and I relaxed, but the trembling continued for several more minutes.

"Where's the person with flaming eyes?" I asked.

"Shh, baby, don't talk," said Mom.

"He was at the house, and loosened the rope, and I saw Aunty in the bathroom praying and crying when I was standing in the cloud with him."

Mom pursed her lips. "Baby, I think it might have been God. Before you woke up, I saw something. It was like … like a cloud covered the bed, and a hand waved over you. Then both of those things disappeared, and you woke up."

After the nurses checked me again, some of my aunts and uncles came to visit.

"We thought we lost you there, little miss," said Aunt Jane.

"You are one miracle child. I think you are meant for something big, young lady. Don't ever forget that," said my Uncle Bill.

Mom tucked the hospital blanket around me, and I winced as it grazed my neck. The whole event already felt like a dream, but the rope burn proved the accident had happened and the man with the flaming eyes … was real.

Stacy sat back, eyebrows raised. "Wow, that's an amazing story. I definitely think God has his hand on your life. No pun intended." She smiled.

I laughed. "My Uncle Bill has always said God has big plans for me because I'm a miracle child. I never disagreed with him, but I've also never been sure what to think about it."

"You know, I believe you saw Jesus." Stacy paused, smiling.

I'd always considered that it might have been an angel, but Jesus? That was new.

Stacy laughed. "I can see you're not so sure about that. Can I share why I believe this?"

"Sure," I said slowly, expecting to hear a sermon.

"There are prophecies that seem to describe Jesus that way. In Revelation it talks about him as a rider on a white horse, whose eyes are like blazing torches, wearing many crowns on his head. And in the book of Daniel, Daniel has a vision where he sees a heavenly man with eyes that look like flaming torches. What do you think about that?" asked Stacy.

I sat back, processing what she said. "Yeah, that is interesting." I didn't know what else to say, but I would definitely be looking those scriptures up when I left.

Stacy smiled. "It will be interesting to see how your life unfolds. Do you want to continue telling your story? We left off with an awful situation."

I cleared my throat. "Yeah, I'm ready to continue."

I stared at the purple plastic of the seat that made part of my bed. It was late morning; the bus was moving, and the buzz of conversation filled the air. Every time steps neared me, I hoped Mom was coming to comfort me, but she never came.

"Edgar, are you sure the shooting had nothing to do with your delivery last night?" asked Becky.

"I'm sure. It was a fight gone bad and we just ended up in the crosshairs. I promise, you don't have to worry about anyone coming after us."

Becky tried to get me up to eat breakfast, but I pretended to be asleep until she left me alone.

Images from the shooting flashed through my mind. Stewart yelling, the wild look in his eyes, calling himself my *savior*, the sound of gunfire. If this was his way of saving people—the traveling, the danger, the crazy rules—I didn't want to be saved. I wanted to go home.

Squeezing my eyes closed, I tried to come up with a plan to run away, but no solution presented itself. Besides, I wasn't sure I could convince Eva to run away with me.

I buried my face in a pillow as hot tears threatened to spill over and sobs forced themselves from my gut. Someone lay down next to me. A sweet, earthy scent reached my nose. Sapphira. Turning over, I hid my face in her shoulder as she hugged me tight.

When I finished crying and stopped breathing in spasms, she pulled away, moved the hair out of my face and kissed my forehead.

"Love you, sis."

I snuggled to her again, wanting to pretend it was only us here. "I love you, too."

The bus stopped. A moment later, Stewart's voice was above us. "Sapphira, quit being lazy and help the women get the laundry. You children stay away from the creek."

Sapphira hugged me tight and whispered in my ear. "Always remember who you are. You have a light in you—don't let it go out. Don't let them take it from you."

I clung tighter to my big sister.

"Let go, I have to get up."

Realizing it would be better for both of us, I released her.

Once everyone left the bus, I listened. Running water—that would be the creek Stewart mentioned—and kids. Sorry, *children*. Stewart insisted the correct term was children because a kid was a baby goat.

Small footsteps creeped toward me, and soon Eva crawled onto the bed. "Are you okay?" she asked.

More tears formed at the question, but I blinked them away, sat up and hugged her. She'd been scared, too, and I felt bad I wasn't able to protect her last night. "Yeah, I'm okay." I sat back and gave her a small smile. Sapphira had been strong for me earlier; now Eva needed me to be strong. "Are you?"

She nodded. "I heard Stewart yelling, but Mom kept her hand on the back of my head so I couldn't see."

"Good." At least Mom could keep *her* safe.

"When the shooting stopped, I saw you at the front of the bus. You didn't move even when Mike came back to the bus and picked you up and carried you to our bed."

"I'm sorry," I said, squeezing her tight.

Looking out the window, I could see we were at another campground. This one was really nice. I could see a playground off in the distance, indoor bathrooms, a laundry room where the women had gone. It looked like there was a swimming pool, too, but it was closed.

Eva sat with me for a while but quickly got bored and wanted me to go outside with her. I didn't want to be anywhere near the others, for fear of someone scolding me for being lazy or not being brave enough last night. But, looking out the window and seeing a campground with lots of trees, I agreed, on condition that we find a tree to climb.

No one paid me any attention as I climbed out of the bus. Part of me was okay with that, and part of me hated them even more.

Thirty minutes of finding zero climbable trees zapped my energy, so I went back to the bus and lay down again.

We spent more than a week at the campground. At night, I tossed and turned. During the day I could focus on the sounds and conversations around me. But when it was dark and quiet, bits and pieces of the shooting played over and over in my mind and refused to stop.

It wasn't until the sun rose and people woke up that I felt I could actually sleep, but Mom got us up for prayer and breakfast. I dragged my feet getting ready and refused to raise my hands during prayer, even though Stewart glared at me and reminded me more than once how important it was to raise our hands.

After breakfast, Stewart canceled the morning meetings and let us go outside. Eva and I headed toward the water to play in the sand and dirt, she with her dolls, and I with my trucks. The air was chilly, but as long as we stayed in the sun, it was warm enough with a light jacket.

I wasn't interested in playing, but I was away from the adults, which, since the shooting, was the only time I felt a sense of safety.

In the evenings, little sparks of light flitted about. Fascinated by them, I asked Mom what they were.

"They're called lightning bugs, baby."

"Can I catch one and keep it?" I asked.

Mom laughed. "No, I don't know what they eat and we don't have a place for it."

On our third day at the campsite, Eva and I were playing a few yards away from the creek. Nearby I heard Mom arguing with Becky. I glanced at them, then returned to digging in the dirt with a stick, keeping my ears open.

"Grace, listen … get out."

"I can't," said Mom.

"… not safe …" Becky's voice trailed off.

"They'll arrest me," Mom said.

"… Might have friends … find a place to…"

Sighing in frustration, I wished I could hear better.

"How? I'll lose … I can't."

More whispering. What could Mom have done that would get her arrested?

"Maybe you'll understand when we get there," said Becky.

122

Her voice sounded closer, and I looked up. She walked toward us and caught my eye.

"Girls, how many times have we told you to stay away from the water? Didn't you learn from the hotel? Get back to the others," she said, swatting the back of my head lightly when I stood. I waited for Eva to get her dolls together before heading back.

"All aboard," yelled Mike. "We heard from Jack, the house came through and we can move in immediately."

Leaving the campground, we drove for several hours, during which we passed a sign that said, "Welcome to Michigan."

We pulled into a long driveway. A large red-brick house stood in the middle of a huge yard. Hope bubbled inside me at the sight of all that space. As soon as Edgar turned off the ignition, I was out the door, running toward the backyard.

"Hey, get back here and help unload this bus," shouted Edgar.

Stopping, I jogged back, grabbed an armload of stuff and headed toward the house. We piled everything in the living room, then Becky gave everyone a job to do. Mine was to carry a bucket of soapy water around and wash the windows. Eva got the job of cleaning baseboards, which meant we had to share the same bucket. Some windows were so big I could only reach halfway up them, but as soon as someone realized this, they found me a short ladder to use. I didn't like the ladder much, since it wobbled, but complaining would only get me harder work, so I kept at it.

When we finished our tasks, Becky told us to clean the floors in the bedrooms upstairs. "There's a broom, mop, and a bucket of water upstairs waiting for you."

Jack and Richard showed up in a mover's van when we'd finished two of the four rooms. Cots, a couch, and other small furniture were unloaded and moved into their designated areas by the men.

Stewart assigned bedrooms to people. Tim stayed with his parents. Eva and I got stuck sleeping on cots in a family room area across from two bedrooms on the second floor. Since we were off

Ol' Yellow, I didn't care that we didn't get a room. We were out of the big ugly bus.

Chapter 16

"Pride equals the downfall of a community. To practice being humble, we need to remember this house is a blessing from God, not gained with our own hands and hard work. Therefore, God has asked us to take this first day in our new home and fast from all food and drink," announced Stewart.

He also laid out the rules for the children. "The basement is off-limits, and during the morning meeting, you'll stay upstairs and do school work until this watch beeps. "Stewart handed me a watch. "When you've completed four hours of times tables, you can go play."

"Are we going to learn anything other than times tables?" I asked.

"No, the government tells public schools what to teach children. Their goal is to train you to believe the U.S. government is a good and legal authority and should be trusted with every part of our lives. Times tables are all you need in life."

Eva and I trudged back upstairs. There was a big picture window on the second floor, overlooking the front lawn. I thought it was too bad it didn't open, or I would throw the watch out.

"Do we really have to do times tables for four hours?" asked Eva.

"No," I said turning around, smiling. "Do you have that deck of cards Grandma gave you?"

Eva grinned, "Yes, I'll go get them."

"Great. Let's play card games. If anyone comes upstairs, we'll say we're using the cards to help us practice. Aces can be ones, jacks can be elevens, queens are twelves, and kings are thirteen. So whatever cards you're holding, you can say you're trying to figure out how to times those numbers."

Eva smiled, ran to her backpack and found the cards. After playing a few rounds of Go Fish, War, and Kings on the Corner, we got bored. I checked the time. We'd only killed two hours.

Eva tried to make a tower from the cards. Good. I pulled out the small knob on the watch and moved the hands forward an hour and a half. If we got in trouble, only I would get punished.

"Let's play Slap Jack."

Eva sighed as her small tower of cards collapsed again. "Okay."

Gathering the cards, I shuffled and counted them out so we each had half the deck. I let Eva win the round so she would want to play again, but as I counted the cards again, the watch beeped. I picked it up and tried to figure out how to make it stop when Becky came upstairs.

"Does that mean we're done?" I asked, holding the still beeping watch out to her.

She took it, made the noise stop, then looked at each of us. "You girls haven't been playing with this, have you?"

Eva shook her head. "No, Sophia came up with a fun game for our times tables. We use the numbers on the cards to make the timeses. We've been playing it this whole time."

"Yeah, do you want to see how it works?"

"Some other time. I guess you can go play now."

We raced downstairs and out the back door. Freedom at last!

We explored every inch of the backyard, including an empty shed near the back of the yard.

"Eva, let's check it out. We could use it as a clubhouse."

Hurrying over, we opened the door.

"Ew, what is that smell?" Eva gagged, which made me laugh, and we both ran out of the shed.

We lay in a pile of leaves and caught our breath.

"What do you think died in there?" Eva asked.

Laughing, I said, "I don't think anything died in there. It smells like rotting food."

"Well, I'm never going near that thing again."

An orange cat with patches of brown and gray on it ran up to us. For the rest of the day it followed us everywhere but wouldn't come in the house. Which was probably a good thing, since it thought our legs made good scratching posts. By evening, our tights had small holes all over them.

In bed that night, we were exhausted, starving, and thirsty.

"I hope we got humbled enough today and get to eat tomorrow," said Eva, snuggling under her blanket. "Do you think Mom will let us have that kitten?"

"I don't know, we can ask tomorrow."

The fast continued the following day. During our free time, we sat under the trees and dozed, because it was the only thing we had energy to do. Before bed that second night, Mom came upstairs to say goodnight to us.

"Girls, your faces are filthy. Come to the bathroom and let's wash them."

We followed her, and when the three of us were in the bathroom, she locked the door, and pulled a sleeve of crackers out from under her shirt.

"Eat quickly," she whispered, opening the package and handing us each a stack of the white squares.

She didn't have to tell us twice; we devoured them, and when we finished, she turned the faucet on and showed us how to cup our hands to catch the cool liquid for drinking.

"Mom," Eva whispered as we sat on the cold tile. "Can we have the kitten out back? Becky said we might have mice. The kitten could eat them and sleep with us."

I looked at Eva, shocked by the lie she told. That was *my* move.

"I'll talk to Edgar. Now, let's get you girls to bed."

Eva winked at me as we walked out of the bathroom, and it filled me with pride.

Mom tucked us in and rejoined the others. As grateful as I was for the food, and happy she'd thought of us, I was mad, too. Mad I didn't think of it first. We could have filled our stomachs with water this whole time. Then we wouldn't have needed Mom to bring the crackers.

For the second night in a row I slept soundly. The next day, Edgar brought the kitten upstairs. "You get to learn responsibility. Both of you will feed and water this cat." Setting it down, he walked away.

"See, I can get my way when I want to." Eva grinned and picked up the orange and gray fluff ball.

"Well done, Eva. What are we going to name it?"

"How about Kitten?"

I shrugged. "That works."

The fast continued, but we had the cat to distract us from empty bellies. I put my idea to the test and quickly changed my mind. The water filled our stomachs but didn't last long, and it made me feel sick. The water sloshed around in my stomach, and the more it moved around, the more sick and weak I was.

Finally, on the fourth day, we woke up to the heavenly smell of toast and eggs.

Eva dressed as fast as possible. "I'm going to eat three plates full," she said, jamming her foot into her shoe.

"Wait, we don't even get seconds, remember? If we run down there, they might make us wait until everyone else has eaten. If we're too excited, we might not look humble."

Eva threw herself back onto her cot, groaning.

"Wait for me to get dressed, then we'll go together, slowly—and don't look too happy. Try not to smile when we get to the kitchen."

"Okay."

I dressed, and we made our way downstairs. Becky had set everything out except for a tray of biscuits Mom was taking out of the oven. Although I knew there was no seasoning, butter, or jam to go on them, my mouth watered. I glanced around to see if anyone would prevent us from getting a plate, but no one paid us any attention, so I motioned to Eva to go ahead.

Grabbing our food, we sat at one of the folding tables. Eva tore a biscuit in half and stuffed most of it in her mouth.

"Try not to eat too fast," I whispered to her. "They might take it away from you."

Bowing her head, she chewed what was in her mouth, then tore off small pieces but shoved them in her mouth at a quick pace.

"Are you trying to get us in trouble?"

She shrugged her shoulders and continued stuffing her face.

After two biscuits and some eggs I was full, but I still wished for seconds.

During the fast, no one had given us a watch and told us to do school work, but today Mike handed it to me and sent us upstairs.

We played card games again, and I changed the time, being careful to move it exactly an hour and a half, so it beeped at the same time as before. When it beeped, Becky appeared and questioned us. She didn't look like she believed our story, but she let us go out to play.

Kitten met us, scratched at our legs, and followed us, even when we climbed the trees. My favorite tree was near the back of the yard. When I was in it, I felt hidden and safe. The house was visible through the branches, which lost more of their leaves every day as winter got closer. The trunk and branches were sturdy, and there was one I could lie flat on. I climbed up the tree during a game of hide and seek, and Eva wasn't able to find me, even when she climbed halfway up searching for me.

That night, Stewart had everyone join in a special time of silent prayer and reflection. He felt each of us should feel very close to God after four days of fasting. "I want each of you to communicate to our most holy Lord how thankful you are. For this house, the food he provides, and the unfolding of God's promised son, who will grow up and be the next leader of our congregation."

I wasn't sure what he meant by that last statement, but Sapphira blushed when he said it. This couldn't be good.

Chapter 17

Exactly one week after arriving at the brick house, I woke up and smiled. But after I'd scanned the surroundings, the smile quickly turned into a frown. *Happy birthday to me.*

The cat jumped on my chest and licked my face. Hugging Kitten close and rolling onto my side, I buried my face in the soft fur and cried.

At home, there would have been cake, presents, playing with friends, and seeing family. Grandma would have given me ten dollars. But I wasn't at home, and I wasn't sure anyone would even remember my tenth birthday. I missed home.

I got up, dressed, headed downstairs for breakfast, and searched the room for Mom. She sat at a table talking with Edgar, Mike, and Becky. I grabbed a plate of food and sat at the table near her, hoping to get her attention, but not once did she look in my direction.

Tim sat on the floor, screaming. "Eggs are yucky! I want pancakes with st-st-stwawbewwies!" The adults didn't seem to notice him either, and eventually he calmed down and fell asleep.

After breakfast, Becky gave me the watch and sent us upstairs. The card games were boring now, but we got them out in case anyone happened to check on us. I made notes in my book and stared out the window while Eva played with Kitten.

Eventually, I tired of staring outside, moved the watch hands forward an hour and a half, and lay on my cot.

"Will you play a game with me? I'm bored," said Eva.

We played a few rounds of Slap Jack until the alarm beeped.

Becky still seemed doubtful about the alarm going off early, but didn't question us again. My plan had worked, and we raced outside to play.

But before we reached the door, Mike stopped us.

"Girls, why are your tights all torn?" he asked.

"The cat keeps scratching at our legs. We try not to let it," I said.

"The cat did this? How about the truth?"

"That is the truth," said Eva. "The holes were smaller, but I guess they got bigger."

He knelt so his head was the same level as mine. "If I find out you girls are lying, I'll have Richard whip you."

Clenching my fists and straightening, I looked him in the eye. "We're. Not. Lying."

"Good." Mike stood and walked away.

That evening, Mom came upstairs instead of going to the meeting. She held two plastic bags and handed one to each of us.

"Happy birthday, Sophia."

A lump formed in my throat. She'd remembered. Inside the bag was a new football. I hugged her and ripped off the cardboard.

"You should have birthdays more often, Sophia," Eva said. "I got a new doll and a board game called Guess Who?'"

That would come in handy during school tomorrow.

"Thanks, Mom, will you stay and play with us?"

"Sure, what do you want to play?"

We showed her the card games we knew, and it almost felt like our Mom was back again. It probably wouldn't last, but I was glad she remembered my birthday.

The following day, Mike took Becky's place as the watch keeper and checker, and our luck ran out.

"Who's changing the time on this?" he asked.

Neither of us answered.

"You girls have an hour and forty-five minutes left of school, and I'm sitting up here to make sure it gets done. So who wants to start?"

Eva struggled with the bigger numbers. Would Mike punish her if she made a mistake?

"I will," I said.

He nodded. "Let's hear 'em."

"One times one is one, one times two is two, one times three is three …"

I pretended to think about the answers to waste time, but eventually I finished, and it was Eva's turn.

She did well with ones, twos, and threes, but got stuck on fours. Mike looked bored. When Eva reached the sixes, she really struggled.

"Remember, it's add—"

"Shut up, she can figure it out herself," said Mike.

Eva finally finished.

Mike nodded at me. "Again."

We both recited the times tables two more times, and the last time I didn't pretend it was hard. School would be over soon, and I hoped Mike would realize what a waste this was.

Finally, we finished and could go outside. I grabbed my football. "Eva, want to play catch?"

Nodding, she grabbed her dolls to play with later, and we headed outside. We played catch for a while, then I climbed into a tree and Eva played dolls. I could see her from my perch. Kitten kept rubbing against her until Eva picked the cat up and put it in her lap, where it stretched, clawing at her tights. I shook my head and climbed down.

Picking up the cat, I sat next to Eva.

"What are we going to do with you, Kitten? You can't keep putting holes in our clothes."

The cat meowed and purred.

"Kitten is so cute, huh Soph?"

"Yes, you are such a cute kitten." I kissed its nose, and set it beside me.

The sky changed from a golden yellow to shades of pale pink and purple.

"Let's head in. It'll be dark soon, and I'm hungry," I said.

Gathering her dolls, Kitten, and the football we started toward the house to put our things away.

Upstairs, Mike was sitting on my cot. Eva and I both stopped at the sight of him.

"Eva, put the cat down," said Mike.

"What are you doing up here?" I asked.

"The three of us need to have a chat." He patted the place next to him. "Come sit."

We sat down, but across from him, on Eva's cot.

"Now, you both told me a cat caused those holes, but both of you like to climb trees. So, let's try this again: How did the holes in your tights get there?"

"The cat scratches at our legs," I said. "It's not the trees."

He frowned and squinted. "I don't like liars." He grabbed Eva's arm and pulled her onto his lap, arms around her waist. Eva's eyes were wide and her lip trembled, but she didn't resist or try to get away.

"Let her go," I demanded.

An evil grin spread across his face and chills raced down my spine.

"You think you're so smart. Changing the time to get out of doing school and making excuses about your clothes." He stuck his nose in Eva's hair, took a deep breath, then slowly licked his lips.

I balled my hands into fists; I would not let him hurt my sister. Eva stared at me but didn't move a muscle.

"Tell the truth," said Mike.

"It was the cat," I said, through clenched teeth.

"Stewart just told me, when your little sister here is of age, she'll be my bride." Grinning again, he grabbed Eva's chin, tilted her head, and slowly licked the side of her face.

Springing forward, I punched him. I punched his face, his shoulder, his neck. I couldn't stop, wouldn't stop. Before I knew what was happening, I was face-down on the floor, with Mike's elbow pressed into the middle of my back. I screamed out in pain and kept screaming as I heard the *thwack, thwack* of the paddle I hadn't seen him holding. My rear end throbbed.

"Maybe now you'll learn to tell the truth," he said.

My tears spilled onto the hardwood floor. "It was the cat!" I yelled as he walked away. I tried to get up, to check on Eva, but my arms were too weak and I was in too much pain. "Eva?" I squeaked out.

A shuffling noise, and she was beside me.

"Did he hurt you?" I asked.

"No, I hid under the cot when he grabbed you. Are you going to be okay?"

I nodded. "Help me get to my bed?"

She helped me stand and held onto my arm until I reached my cot. I lay face-down on it, and she handed me Wooby, then sat next to me and stroked my hair.

"Why did he do that?" asked Eva.

"Because he's evil." I buried my face in Wooby and cried until there were no more tears.

Chapter 18

6 Months Before The FBI Standoff

"Beloved family, today is a day of Thanksgiving, and I have a word from the Lord," said Stewart as he wrapped up prayer time. He had that crazy look in his eyes again.

"Not only has our gracious Lord followed through on his promise to provide new life to our community through my beautiful bride Jasmine, your new prophetess, but he's provided a bountiful meal because of our faithfulness in fasting last week, which Mike and Becky got for us earlier this week. The women will prepare our feast, and I expect the children to clean the house today so the men can rest."

After prayer, Sam walked up to me and Eva and shoved a paper into my hands, with writing on both sides. "Stewart wanted me to give this to you. It's everything that needs cleaning, and our faces better shine in the floor." He chuckled and walked off.

I stared at the long list of chores.

"Come on, Eva, let's get started. Maybe Tim can help a little."

We headed to the kitchen to grab supplies from the broom closet by the back door. I grabbed the mop and bucket and handed them to Eva, then tried to reach for the window cleaner and dust spray, but they were just out of my reach.

"Here, let me help you with that," said Jack from behind me.

I moved out of the way as much as I could while Jack squeezed into the small space and grabbed the items I needed. "Is there anything else you need from those top shelves?" he asked, setting the supplies on the table.

"No, I don't think so. Thank you."

He smiled. "Let me know if you need anything later, I'll be around."

Eva and I had hauled our cleaning supplies to the living room and were looking over the list to make a plan on where to begin when the doorbell rang. The strangeness of the sound made everyone freeze. We never had visitors.

Jack answered the door.

"Hi, can I help you?" Glancing at me and Eva, he stepped outside, leaving the door open just wide enough that his body blocked the opening. But I was close enough to hear the conversation.

"Hello, I'm Officer Martin, this is Officer Fen and Miss Hope from Child Protective Services. A family member has requested a welfare check for Eva Wilkins. Is Grace Wilkins available?"

"I believe so, can you wait here a moment? I'll go get her," Jack said.

"Of course."

Jack stepped back into the house, closed the door and locked it. "Someone has requested a welfare check for Eva. They'll want to talk to all the children."

"Sam, take Tim downstairs to Sapphira and make sure they both stay there," said Stewart. "Grace, I'm sure you'll be able to manage Eva so she says only what she should."

Mom nodded and headed to the door. Everyone else went back to what they'd been doing before, except Jack, who walked toward me, smiling, and placed his hand on my shoulder, squeezing slightly. "Since you've lost a helper for a few minutes, why don't I help you? We can start in the kitchen."

"Hello, I'm Grace Wilkins. How can I help you?"

Ignoring Jack's attempt at distraction for the moment, I leaned around him and listened.

"We've been asked to do a welfare check on your daughter Eva. You and your daughter need to come to the station. Eva's father, Isaac, is there and would like to see her."

Dad found us! I couldn't keep the grin off my face.

"Sophia, we really should get started on the cleaning. The list is pretty long," said Jack.

"Eva, please go get your shoes on," said Mom, being careful not to open the door too wide. My chances of seeing my stepdad were slipping away.

Eva obeyed but didn't seem as excited at the prospect of seeing her dad again as I was.

I looked up at Jack. "Can you carry the mop?"

"Absolutely," he said, placing his hand on my back, guiding me away from the door.

I turned and ducked under his arm, dashing to the door. "What about me, Mom? I want to see Dad, too," I said, standing next to her so the officers could see me. The male policeman who'd introduced himself as Officer Martin smiled.

"Any other children in the home will need to come, too," said the female officer.

I guessed she was Officer Fen, since the other woman wasn't wearing a police uniform.

Mom's shoulders slumped, and she sent me to get my shoes on, too. But I didn't want to leave Sapphira behind. "Should I get Sapphira, too?" I asked, as innocently as possible.

Mom's lips tightened, and she looked over her shoulder at Stewart. "Yes, go get her, please." Stewart stood in the middle of the living room, glaring at me. His mouth worked back and forth and spit bubbles were gathering in the corners, but I ignored him and ran downstairs. With luck, we'd never see these people again.

"Sapphira, you have to come with us to the police station. Mom told me to come get you." She'd been sitting on a bed with Tim, looking at a picture book.

"Okay, I'll be right there. Tim, you need to stay down here. I'll leave the book here for you to look at. Be a good boy."

Sapphira stepped outside and the three visitors glanced at her, then at each other. What did they see? I eyed my sister but didn't notice anything strange about her appearance.

The four of us climbed into one of the officer's cars and we headed to the station.

There, we were escorted to a room with a brown desk and four folding chairs.

"Girls, I'm Officer Martin, and this is Miss Hope. We'll get you all checked out by a doctor and ask you some questions about where you're living. Grace, we understand Isaac is only the biological father of Eva, is that correct?"

"Yes, that's right."

"Great. Eva, come with me and we'll go see your dad," said Miss Hope.

"Sapphira, while Eva is visiting with her dad, I'd like to ask you some questions in another room," said Officer Martin.

"I would like to go with my daughter while you question her," said Mom.

Officer Martin looked at Sapphira. "How old are you, sweetheart?"

"Fourteen."

"Sapphira is old enough to choose if she wants a parent present or not. What would you prefer, Sapphira?"

My older sister bit her lip and shifted her eyes between the officer, Mom, and the floor. "I think I would rather go by myself," she mumbled.

"Very good. We shouldn't be too long," said Officer Martin.

"Can I see Dad, too?" I asked as they headed toward the door. Mom put a hand on my knee.

"We'll let you see him soon."

"Officer Martin?" The policewoman, Officer Fen, who'd been at the house, met them just outside the room. "The young girl, Eva, says she doesn't know Isaac."

There was a pause. Officer Martin stuck his head in the door again. "Sophia, why don't you come see your stepdad now."

140

I smiled, jogged toward the door, and followed Officer Fen to another room. Dad and Eva were there. His light brown hair was longer than I remembered it being, and he had the beginnings of a beard.

"Eva, that's enough, you know who I am. Get over here and give me a hug," said Isaac.

Eva hung back, hesitating.

I walked up to her. "Eva, that's Dad. It's okay."

Eva gave a sheepish smile and opened her arms toward Dad, who immediately picked her up and hugged her tight.

"That's my girl. I've missed you so much." Then he put Eva down and looked at me. "Sophia." He smiled and opened his arms. Lunging toward him, I let him wrap me in his big, strong, safe arms. After a moment he released me, held my shoulders and looked at me. "How are you doing? Are you okay?"

I could see the concern in his green eyes. Dark circles were under them. He looked tired. How I wanted to tell him everything, but I couldn't get the words past the lump in my throat. I nodded and hugged him again.

They allowed us to visit with him for about thirty minutes. After that, they took us to a room where a doctor did a basic checkup, looking at our eyes, ears, and throat, and checking our heart and lungs. When that was finished, we returned to the room where Mom and Sapphira waited for us.

"Everything looks like it's in order here. We'll have Officer Fen take you home," said Miss Hope.

Disappointment filled me. Why couldn't we go with Dad? Walking out to the car, Isaac stopped us. "Grace, I'd like to take you and the girls out to dinner tomorrow and buy them some new clothes."

"I don't think that's a good idea," said Mom.

"Please, Grace, it's just dinner and shopping. I miss my girls."

Mom looked at each of us. "I'll think about it."

Isaac took a piece of paper out of his pocket and handed it to her. "Here is the number of the hotel where I'm staying. Call me and let me know."

Mom took the paper, and we climbed into the police car.

Back at the house, Stewart met us at the door. "Sapphira, you've had a long morning. I want you to go downstairs and rest. Grace, I'd like to talk to you. Girls, you still have chores to complete. I expect you to finish the list I gave you."

The cleaning supplies still sat in the middle of the living room. I had hoped I'd be able to talk to Eva about seeing Dad. Her pretending not to know him worried me, but Stewart had told us several times to forget everyone we used to know. I'd tried to protect Eva from everything they said and did, and I was afraid Eva really was forgetting our family back home.

But I didn't get the chance to talk about it because Jack was glued to my side—holding the stepladder while I washed the windows, getting me clean rags, and asking a lot of questions about our morning at the police station.

"Are you okay? Were you scared to go to the police station? Did you get to see your stepdad?" Those were just a few of the questions he asked. I noticed he didn't ask about Eva's or Sapphira's experience, just mine. I kept my answers short, figuring he would tell Stewart everything.

Jack stayed with us the whole time we cleaned and helped us put all the supplies away. By that time, dinner was ready. As I headed upstairs to wash my hands, Jack stopped me by placing his hand on my shoulder.

"I know the others can be hard on you children, but you don't have to be afraid of me. When the timing is right, I'll take good care of you."

Chills ran down my spine but I smiled at him. "I'm not afraid of you, Jack."

He squeezed my shoulder and smiled back. "Good, because I think we'll make a great team."

Chapter 19

Pacing the living room, I listened as hard as I could. Isaac had showed up at the house, asking Mom to let him take us all to dinner tonight. After a short argument about how Isaac should have waited for Mom to call, Stewart invited him in, and the three sat at the kitchen table. We were sent upstairs and not allowed down until their conversation was done.

Occasionally, I heard raised voices but couldn't make out any of the conversation. After an hour, we were allowed downstairs again.

"Girls, Isaac is taking us and your sister Sapphira out to dinner tonight. Go get ready," said Mom.

"Can we get McDonald's?" asked Eva as we left the house.

"Absolutely," said Isaac. "I think I saw one with a playground, too."

Eva clapped her hands. On the drive, she chattered about all the food she would order.

"Sounds like your eyes are bigger than your stomach, little girl," said Isaac. "Why don't you pick your favorite thing first? If you're still hungry when you finish, I'll order something else for you."

At the restaurant we ordered and sat down. "Sophia, let's play while our food cooks," said Eva.

I shook my head. "I want to stay with Dad."

"Okay, if that's what you want," she said and ran off to play.

Isaac smiled and watched her go, but his eyes looked sad.

"I still wish you'd waited until I called you," said Mom.

"Would you have called?"

143

Mom pursed her lips and didn't respond.

"That's what I figured. And after that … *discussion* with Stewart, I think you and the girls should come home with me. Today. We'll have the police go back to the house. You can pack your things—it doesn't look like you have a lot—and we'll leave. All the legal stuff we were going through before you left, we'll drop it. Just let me take you all home."

Sapphira sat next to me, staring at her hands and saying nothing.

"It's not that easy, Isaac, and I don't think we should talk about this in front of the girls," said Mom.

"Fine, but answer one question. Do you think the girls are safe? I mean, really safe, with these people?"

Mom cleared her throat and stared at the table. "If I didn't think they were safe, we would have left long ago."

I didn't think Mom was telling the truth, and I think Dad knew it, too, because he looked at me, his eyebrows raised. I rolled my eyes and shook my head.

Conversation stopped until the food arrived, and because Eva was at the table, Isaac tried to keep things upbeat. He made silly faces to make us laugh and told some of his best jokes.

When it was time to leave, I hoped Mom would change her mind and let Dad take us home, but neither of them mentioned the idea again. Instead, Dad asked if he could take us shopping.

"Not tonight. It's been a long couple of days, and Sapphira hasn't been feeling well."

I realized Sapphira hadn't said much of anything. She had always loved talking to Dad back home.

"Tomorrow, then?" asked Isaac.

"I can't, I have things to do," said Mom.

We pulled up to the house. "Let me take the girls, then. I can pick them up in the morning and have them back by lunch."

Mom climbed out of the car, shaking her head. "Come on, girls."

Isaac put the car in park and shut it off, climbing out, too. "Grace, please. I head home the day after tomorrow. Just let me spend time with my daughter."

He wasn't really going to leave without us. He would convince Mom to take us with him. He had to.

"Sapphira, Sophia, Eva, go into the house," Mom ordered.

We obeyed, but I dawdled, hoping to hear Mom's final decision, but she watched and waited until we were all inside.

A few minutes later, Mom came in. She didn't make eye contact with me but walked to the kitchen where the other adults were.

The next morning, someone gently shook me awake.

"Wake up, girls, your mom is letting me take you to buy clothes."

I opened my eyes, and Isaac smiled down at me. Was I dreaming? Eva sat up on her cot, rubbing her eyes.

I stretched and yawned. It didn't feel like a dream.

"Hurry and get dressed and meet me downstairs, before she changes her mind." He winked at me. It was a joke, but I hurried anyway.

Mom and Sapphira didn't come with us. At first, I took my time trying on clothes, but I'd always hated clothes shopping and soon Isaac and I were waiting on Eva. She tried on outfit after outfit, prancing out of the fitting room and twirling with a hand on her hip to show off each one.

Dad's face lit up as Eva warmed up to him. He had his little girl back. Isaac and I didn't talk much, but that was okay. It was enough to be near him. Eventually, Isaac told Eva it was time to go, and I couldn't help but ask what had been on my mind since we first saw him at the police station.

"Are you going to take us back home to Utah soon?"

Dad wrapped his arm around me and kissed the top of my head. "I wish I could, sweetie. As much as I disagree with how things are, it is best to follow the law. Now that I know where you girls are, I hope it won't take too long to get you all home safely."

On the walk back to the car, Eva pointed out a black man walking into the store. "Dad, did you know God cursed black people?"

He looked at me. "No, I didn't know that. Why are they cursed?"

"Because they disobeyed God."

"Who told you that?" asked Isaac.

"Hannah. She doesn't live with us anymore."

On the drive back, Eva talked non-stop about what she'd learned since we'd left home. She talked about raising our hands during prayer, why women did all the cooking and cleaning, and even reasons Stewart had given for why we had to fast. It surprised me she'd picked up on so much. She never talked about it with me, probably because she figured I already knew.

Dad's face grew more worried the more she talked, but he tried to keep smiling. When he dropped us off at the house, he hugged us both for a long time.

"I'll try to come back and visit as soon as I can."

Next time, I hoped it wouldn't just be a visit. I wanted to go home.

Heading upstairs to put my new clothes away, I thought I heard Sapphira crying. Moving toward the sound, I heard Stewart's voice, then Sapphira sobbing.

Rushing to the bedroom door the sound came from, I threw it open. My whole body tensed. Stewart and Sapphira were on the bed, Stewart on top of her, pinning her down with his knees. In his hand he held a blade to her throat—an actual sword.

"Tell me what you said to the police," threatened Stewart.

The door banged against the wall, and they both looked in my direction.

Tears stained Sapphira's bright red face, and her stomach looked strange and swollen. This wasn't right. What should I do? I stared at them, taking in the whole picture.

"Leave her alone!" I shouted.

"Get out of here, child. Now!" said Stewart.

"Please go," mouthed Sapphira.

Her red, tear-stained face made my blood boil. How could I leave her like that? But what help could I give? Jack came up behind me. He'd always been nice; he would do something. But his face was stern.

Grabbing my arm, he pulled me away from the room. "Stay put."
Returning to the bedroom he closed the door.

I didn't stay there but ran to find Mom. She could fix this.
"Mom!" I screamed, "Mom, where are you?"

I found her in the front yard, talking to Edgar and Sam.

"Mom ... Sapphira ..." I grabbed her arm and pulled on it, trying
to catch my breath.

"What's wrong? What about Sapphira?" asked Mom.

"Stewart ... has a sword ... to her throat," I gasped.

"What? Where?" said Mom, running into the house behind me.
"Upstairs."

"Go find Eva and stay in the backyard," she commanded.

On the way, I saw the others gathering in the living room.

Richard tried to block Mom from going upstairs. "She is his
wife. You no longer have any say over her."

"Get out of my way, or you'll regret it," she said, pushing past
him.

I obeyed Mom, because these people would probably blame or
punish me for what was happening. Finding Eva in the kitchen, I
dragged her out the back door.

"What's going on?" she asked.

"I'm not sure, but Mom is really mad."

It wasn't a lie. I had no clue why Stewart would hold a sword to
Sapphira's throat, why no one would help Sapphira, or what Mom
would do.

An hour passed before Edgar came out to check on us. "Are you
girls all right?"

"Yes, but it's getting cold out here. Can we go inside?" I asked.

"I suppose it wouldn't hurt, but stay downstairs for now."

Eva skipped into the house and I could hear her asking Becky for
something to eat before the door closed.

"Is Sapphira okay?" I asked, walking back beside Edgar.

"*Jasmine* is fine," said Edgar, stressing her new name.

"Can I talk to her?"

"She's sleeping right now. Maybe later."

"Mom said Sapphira hasn't been feeling well, and her stomach is swollen. Is she sick?"

Edgar smiled. "No, your sister's pregnant."

I thought back to Sapphira and Stewart's wedding. Kids at school had talked about how babies were made, giggling and making disgusted noises as they did, but I couldn't imagine Sapphira and Stewart kissing or … other stuff. I shuddered. My sister was too young to have a baby. Only adults had babies. How had this happened? Did Mom know?

These questions swirled around in my brain as I walked into the house. Sam and Richard were sitting at the kitchen table. They looked up at me when I walked inside, and their gaze was not friendly. Becky was at the stove cooking, and Eva stood nearby, practically drooling.

Mom stood at the front door in the living room, looking upset. Figuring it must be Isaac at the door, I walked up next to Mom but was surprised to find *my* dad, Dennis, standing there.

Mom shoved me back.

"No, you can't take Sophia. Get out of here," she shouted, slamming the door shut.

"What was he doing here?" I asked.

Mom threw her hands in the air. "I don't think even Dennis knows why he showed up here. It's been a long day already. I'm going to go lay down. Keep your sister quiet, okay?"

She left before I could respond. Isaac was more of a dad to me than my own. Dennis hadn't been part of my life until he met his new wife, Paula. I was pretty sure she was the one who had talked my dad into visiting me more often. I looked out the window to see if he was still on the front porch, but he'd gone.

"Everyone—in the living room now, we need to have a meeting," bellowed Stewart. "We have had far too many government visitors over the past few days. Edgar, I need you to make arrangements with your militia contacts to get everyone out of here safely."

"Stewart, forgive me, but I'm not comfortable staying here for another night with Child Protective Services lurking about. I'm getting my family out tonight. We can meet up with the rest of you at a later date," said Mike.

"I understand, brother. Go in peace," Stewart said.

Mike picked up three backpacks and Becky lifted Tim into her arms. They headed out the back door.

"Jack, you've done a great job finding us new places to live. Work with Edgar to come up with solutions," said Stewart.

Police sirens sounded outside, and everyone turned to look out the front window. Two police cars pulled up out front. One blocked the driveway, the other parked in the grass.

"What should we do, Stewart?" asked Sam.

"Everyone stay calm. Grace, take your two youngest upstairs and stay with them."

The police knocked on the door. I watched from the top of the stairs as Stewart answered the door.

"Hi, we're here to follow up on the welfare check for Eva Wilkins and to discuss Sapphira Wolf's test results with her and her mother. We just need to check out the house and make sure everything is okay inside."

I couldn't see the police officer, but he sounded friendly enough. Stewart didn't respond at first.

"Why the sirens and lights?" asked Stewart.

"Just a precaution. Welfare checks can be stressful for parents, and a lot of times they try to run. Usually that only happens when they know they've done something wrong, though."

Stewart stood in the doorway a moment longer but then opened the door wider and invited the police officers inside.

"Someone from CPS should be here shortly. Mind if we look around?" asked the officer.

Stewart nodded. Three police officers walked around the first floor, opening doors and checking out each room. Finishing the main floor, two officers checked out the basement.

"Nice place you have here," said the police officer, rocking back and forth on his feet, hands resting on his utility belt. Jack smiled at him. When the other two officers returned, they came upstairs and checked all the bedrooms.

As they finished, a woman in a black pantsuit stepped into the house. I recognized her as Miss Hope.

The three officers greeted her, and they huddled together and whispered a few minutes.

Finally, their circle broke up and they asked to speak with Sapphira. She joined them, and again they whispered, but Sapphira kept shaking her head. One officer stood behind her.

"What are they doing, Mom?" I asked.

"I'm not sure, baby. Stay here, I'll go find out."

"Mommy, please don't let them take me!" screamed Sapphira.

Two of the officers held Sapphira under her arms and were forcing her to walk out the door. Miss Hope rushed over to Mom, who had run down the stairs, blocking her from getting to Sapphira.

I crouched, not wanting them to see me, in case they tried to take me, too.

Mom reached her hands toward Sapphira as the officers walked her out of the house. "My baby! Where are you taking her?"

"What's going on? You can't take her without a warrant. I demand to see a warrant," shouted Stewart.

"Are you Stewart Warden?" asked one policeman.

"Yes, and I demand to see a warrant."

The officer pulled a piece of paper from his back pocket, unfolded it and held it up in front of Stewart's face. "Stewart Warden, you are under arrest for the rape of a minor."

Stewart raised his arms in the air and turned his back on the policeman. "See, my children? Here is proof of how cruel the American government is. They have no concern for our best interests. They want to shut us down. Take away our children, separate families, and keep us from setting up God's kingdom here on Earth."

Stewart quickly paced the length of the house as he shouted. The crazy, wild look returned to his eyes. Eva joined me at the top of the stairs but soon retreated to her cot and hid under her blanket. The others lined the walls and watched their leader with concerned looks.

Stewart stopped in front of Edgar and pointed his long, bony finger in his face. "You. You brought me my wife. Young, sweet, and beautiful ..."

The spit gathering and bubbling at the corners of his mouth made me want to barf. I'd never seen someone foam at the mouth; I'd only heard of dogs doing this. Did he have rabies?

"She's gone from me," moaned Stewart, "stolen by the enemies of our collective and holy happiness."

Two more officers entered the house, and Stewart pointed at them. "Get out! You've done your damage, you can't have the others." Stewart looked at Mom. "Take your other two children and leave here. These government pigs will return for them—the angel of the Lord is speaking now. Take them, protect them, and when we find a permanent place for our holy community, you can return to us with two young women, ready to be brides. Ready to expand our community."

"Stewart Warden, put your hands in the air and kneel on the ground. You are under arrest for child abuse and statutory rape. Anything you say or do can and will be used against you in a court of law."

Stewart raised his hands, but did not kneel. "The law? The unfair law of the American government who only desires to squelch the religious freedoms of our community? What lawyer would defend me? They are all paid by the government."

"Sir, kneel on the ground, hands behind your head."

"I kneel to no man who—"

Both officers sprang toward Stewart, grabbing his arms and forcing him to the ground. Handcuffing him, they hauled him out of the house. Stewart continued screaming about the injustices of the government all the way to the car.

Chapter 20

"How did your stepdad, Isaac, find you?" asked Stacy.

"I asked him about that recently, and he said he'd been trying to track us down since we left. Sapphira's uncle, Paul, helped him with funds and even hired an investigator to help with the search.

"Isaac figured out we were in Michigan, but wasn't sure where. He stopped at a restaurant for some breakfast and happened to see Mike and Becky. This was right before Thanksgiving, when they were out getting food for our dinner. He recognized Becky because she'd hung around our house in Utah when Edgar and Mom first got married.

"The sight of Becky told him he was close, so he went to the local police station, told them who he was and that he was trying to find us. They told him they were familiar with our group and had been keeping an eye on us for some time but hadn't found a reason to investigate.

"He requested the child welfare check, which gave them the permission they needed to come to the house."

"Wow, that's incredible. What did Sapphira tell the police?"

"I'm not positive, but I know she agreed to take a pregnancy test, even though she was showing. I don't know if she told the police Stewart got her pregnant, or if something slipped when Stewart, Mom, and Isaac had that heated discussion in the kitchen."

Stacy leaned back in her chair. "That must have been hard, seeing your sister taken away like that."

"What bothered me the most was them separating us and not knowing if I would ever see her again."

"That makes sense. How are you doing right now? Do you need to take a break?"

I took a deep breath. "I think I'm okay."

"Okay. What happened with the rest of the group after Stewart's arrest?"

"Well, as far as I know, Mike, Becky, and Tim got away before the police showed up. Once the police left with Sapphira and Stewart, Sam took off. I remember him saying he wouldn't stick around if our family stayed in the community, because he'd always suspected we would bring them trouble.

"Jack and Richard stuck around. Working with Edgar to contact militia people for a new house. Jack told Edgar about a safe house we could use until we could join them again. I only know this because Mom told me years later. We left Jack and Richard that evening, and arrived at the safe house in the middle of the night."

I woke up when the car stopped moving, and at first I didn't know where I was. It was so dark I couldn't see my hand in front of my face. One of the front doors shut softly, and a moment later a small, bright light shone through the window. It was Edgar, holding a flashlight in his hand. Now I could see the car was parked in a driveway.

He opened the door and stuck his head inside. "The lights don't work. We have to unpack in the dark, so be careful where you step. You'll be able to see better in the house."

Climbing out and carrying our things inside, we found the rooms set up as though someone already lived here. A red leather couch in the living room had a small blanket crumpled in one corner, as though someone had used it while watching TV, then tossed it aside. The walls were bare of decoration throughout the house. The kitchen had a fridge and stove, but of course we wouldn't be able to use them if the power was off.

Upstairs were three bedrooms, all with beds that had sheets and blankets on them. It was weird. Where were the people who lived here? It was clean, not like the big brick house that we'd had to clean before it was livable.

"The room on the right is for me and your mom. You girls can pick from the other two," said Edgar.

Eva and I smiled at each other and ran to the bedrooms. The light of a rising full moon filtered through the windows on this side of the house, making it easier to see. The first room contained a small bed, a blue dresser, and an orange toy chest. Eva busied herself with the toys while I checked out the other room. As soon as I peeked in from the doorway, I turned around and walked away. Something was wrong with that room. It had a bed similar to the other one, but rumpled sheets and blankets covered it. There was a green dresser on the far wall and a table next to the bed, but no toy chest.

A dark stain covered the thin carpet in one corner, like something had spilled there. A lot of something. And since I had the creepy crawlies, I decided it was probably blood. I would find out in the morning, but sleeping in there was out of the question.

"Did you girls decide?" asked Mom.

"Can we both sleep in the other room? I don't like this one."

Edgar walked up beside Mom, "Well, then Eva can stay in that one."

My heart nearly leaped into my throat. I couldn't let that happen. "Why can't we stay together?"

"Because I said so. You girls get separate rooms here," said Edgar.

Eva glanced into the creepy room, then at me. "I like the other one better."

Obviously I wouldn't convince anyone, and I definitely didn't want my little sister to sleep in there, so I agreed to take the scary room.

I might have tried moving to the couch after everyone fell asleep, but I thought there might be other scary rooms I didn't know about yet. It wasn't worth the risk. Climbing into bed, I pulled the covers up to my chin. They smelled old, like they needed washing. I imagined that the body of the person who lost all that blood had lain here. I imagined a lifeless form lying in the bed I occupied, covered in flies and maggots. Why did my brain go there?

Scrambling out of the bed, I shook the blankets and carefully checked the sheets and pillows for any signs of bugs as best I could in the dim light. When I finally convinced myself the bed wasn't covered in bugs, I lay down again and imagined myself high in a tree until I fell asleep.

I dreamed about a little boy standing at the edge of my bed in the dark. He did not move; he just stared at me. I could have sworn he was trying to talk to me, but nothing came out. He had black hair that was the same length all the way around his head, not quite long enough to touch his ears. He wore a dark blue shirt and dark colored shorts. What scared me most was the slit in his throat. I kept trying to get away and was unable to move. My body was paralyzed.

I woke up in a sweat. Sun shone through the window, and I stared at the blinds, listening to the pounding of my heart. I wanted to run out of the room, but I couldn't move. My limbs seemed frozen, and I focused on trying to bend my fingers.

As soon as I managed that task, I tested the rest of my limbs before climbing out of bed and running to the doorway.

Mom and Edgar weren't awake yet, and neither was Eva. Unsure of what I could do, I lingered in the doorway and stared at the spot on the floor. The carpet was a dark forest green color, but the stain looked black.

Gathering my courage, I went in, knelt on the carpet and inspected the spot. It looked like the shadow of a puddle. Running my fingers over the spot, I cringed. The fibers stuck together, as though the blood had soaked into the carpet and dried before anyone tried to clean it.

A bullet casing peeked out between the baseboard and the carpet. It took a few seconds of wiggling it back and forth before I could get it out. Later, I would have to ask Edgar what kind it was.

I explored every inch of that room and found bullet casings everywhere. Picking some up, I turned them over in my fingers. Whatever gun they came from, it was big. The little boy being murdered wasn't an impossible idea. Would the killers come back? I ran out to see if anyone else was awake yet.

Mom and Edgar's voices traveled upstairs from below. Should I go down? They were praying. I would rather not. Instead, I stayed upstairs, wandering from room to room, and occasionally peeking downstairs. I found more bullet casings; they were everywhere. I kept some for my treasure collection and wrote down my theories of how they got there in my notebook.

The house was oddly quiet, since it was only the four of us, and every creak of the floorboards made me jump.

"Sophia? Where are you?" asked Eva.

"Here," I said, walking out of the bathroom. "Finally, you're awake. I've been waiting forever."

"Girls, breakfast is in the cooler we brought from the other house. Help yourselves to it, but that's it for today. I'll get more food tonight," yelled Mom.

"If you go outside to play, try to be quiet. We don't want to draw attention to ourselves. Also, the water is shut off, so the bathroom is out by the back fence," said Edgar.

"We have to go potty outside? That's gross," said Eva.

"It's not so bad," I said. "The hard part is making sure you don't get your pants wet."

Eva frowned as we headed for the food. It had been a long time since we'd been allowed to choose what to eat, so this was a treat. I picked a bunch of grapes, some cheese, and a slice of bread. Since it came from the other place, it was still healthy stuff, but hopefully Edgar would pick up something good. Back in Utah, I'd seen him eat candy bars and drink soda all the time.

"Do we have school?" asked Eva as we finished eating.

"No, not while we're here," said Mom.

I gave Eva a high-five, and we ran out back to explore. A thick layer of leaves covered the yard. We waded through them, picked them up, and tossed them into the air.

Toward the side of the house was a chicken coop. We both thought it would make a great clubhouse, but as we neared, three chickens came out and surprised us. It was another sign people had lived here recently. What happened, and where were they? Running inside, I told Mom and Edgar about the chickens. Who knows how long they'd been here without food or water.

"Yes, I know about the chickens. Don't get too attached. They'll be our dinner soon," said Edgar.

Eva would probably cry when I told her. "Do we need to feed them?" I asked.

Edgar looked through the cabinets in the kitchen, found a small bag of feed and handed it to me. "One handful for each of you girls, they don't need much."

I nodded and ran back outside. We threw the grain at the chickens, then watched them peck at it.

"They're so cute," said Eva.

"Edgar says we can't get too attached to them."

"Why not?"

I sighed, placed my hands on her shoulders and looked her in the eyes. "I know you won't like this, but I'm going to tell you, because I want to prepare you, okay?"

She nodded, her eyes wide.

"We might have to eat them."

The corner of her lips turned down, and she looked at the chickens again, then back at me. "But I named them."

"Well, take the names back."

She turned to the chickens, tears gathering in her eyes. "Sorry, Whitey, Brownie, and Lucy, but I can't name you, so I'm taking the names back and will just call you chickens. I won't tell you why, because you might get scared."

I rolled my eyes. "Come on, let's explore the rest of the yard."

"Hey girls, do you want to help me rake up all these leaves? Afterwards you can jump in the piles. It'll be fun," Edgar interrupted.

Eva and I looked at each other and laughed. "Okay!" we both said enthusiastically.

We found a rake, and Edgar helped us make huge leaf piles that we jumped and hid in. After giving us a chance to play in the leaves for a while, Edgar asked us to help him put all the leaves in bags.

"Great job, girls," he said when the job was done. "Let's go get some lunch." We grabbed food from the cooler just as someone walked into the kitchen, and I jumped. It was Mom. She had a blank look on her face, as if she was deep in thought.

"Mom?"

"Yeah, baby?"

"Did you see the carpet stain in my room?"

"No."

"I think it's a bloodstain from someone getting killed."

Mom laughed. "I'm sure it's nothing that dramatic. Let's go look."

Leading the way, I walked confidently, convinced she would agree with me once she saw the spot. Reaching the room, I pointed to the spot.

Mom inspected it for a few moments. "That looks like punch, not blood."

Disappointed, I said, "Why can't I sleep with Eva? I don't like this room. It's creepy."

"You girls have been cooped up together so much, you need to have your own space. If you don't want to sleep in here, trade with Eva. She only likes the other room because of the toy box. Move it in here, and I'm sure she'll happily move with it."

After watching my big sister get dragged off, I really didn't want my own space. I wanted to keep Eva close, so I could protect her, or at the very least, make sure we stayed together if someone came to take either of us away.

Without Stewart and the others here, we had more freedom. Wondering how far this new freedom would reach, I explored every room in the house. No one yelled at me or told me I couldn't go into them. There weren't any clothes in the closets or dressers, and no food in the kitchen.

Since the house wasn't all shot up, experts must have shot the guns. Maybe the people who lived here practiced shooting inside. Then someone snuck in and killed the little boy in the bedroom, but the rest of the family got out.

No, that didn't explain why their clothes and food were gone. Maybe they heard about an attack, so they got ready to run, but someone got in, killed the boy, and the others ran. That would also explain why the blood would have been on the floor for a while before being cleaned up.

That night, when Mom told us to go to bed, I stood at the door. I needed my pajamas, so I ran in, grabbed them, and ran out, then changed in the bathroom. Mom would make me switch with Eva if I didn't sleep in there; I had to protect her from whatever evil thing was in that room.

Taking a deep breath, I ran and jumped onto the bed, and covered my whole body, including my head, with the blanket. Then I tried to think about all the fun I'd had that day, instead of the room and the murdered boy.

Chapter 21

Prayer and super-healthy food were a thing of the past. Edgar bought Pop Tarts, granola bars, fruit snacks, bottled water and other packaged foods, and it all tasted amazing. On top of that, we got to sleep in as much as we wanted. Since the power was out, cooking was out of the question unless we made a fire outside, and we couldn't store anything in the fridge.

Sticky dirt covered my hands, and I rubbed them together and watched it flake off as Eva and I sat near the coop while the chickens pecked at the ground. During the day, it was easy to ignore the itchy, crackly feel of my skin. But at night it only added a layer of spookiness to the haunted room, as I thought of bugs feeding on my blood.

"Sophia, I don't like this house. How long do you think we'll stay here?" asked Eva.

"I don't know. Mom and Edgar leave every morning. I'm sure they're looking for a new place to live." That was only a guess, though. For all I knew, we would live here until Mom thought it was safe to join the others again. Or until we reached "womanhood" and we were forced to marry Richard, Mike, Sam, or Jack. "We have to keep making the best of it. If we try to have fun, the time will pass faster," I said.

"Yeah, you're right. Do you think Sapphira is okay?"

It was a question I asked myself constantly. I hoped they'd taken her home. "I'm sure she is. She probably has lots to eat, and new clothes. If anything, she's probably worried about us. In fact, I bet she's back home with Dad."

"I hope so," said Eva.

We hated being at the house by ourselves, especially with the creepy room, so we tried to keep ourselves busy, playing downstairs or going outside. If it rained or snowed, we took our blankets and sleeping bags and made a fort in the living room. We would pretend to be explorers in the wilderness and search all over the house, minus the scary room, to find clues, and used the discarded shotgun shells as our treasure.

One morning I woke suddenly, breathing hard as though I'd had a nightmare, but I didn't remember having one. My body wasn't numb, like it had been when I dreamed about the ghost boy, and I jumped out of bed and raced down the hall to Mom and Edgar's room. It was empty. I heard the floorboards downstairs creak, hurried down, and found them getting ready to leave. I realized it was probably their movements that woke me up, but I still didn't want them to leave us alone.

"Please, Mom, don't go," I begged.

"I have to go, baby. Edgar and I have a job today and we can't miss it, or we won't have food to eat." She kissed me on the cheek. "Behave, and watch after your sister."

There was no arguing with that. "I always do," I said as they left. I walked over to the chair by the window, staring out of the frost covered glass as they drove off. A thin layer of snow covered the ground outside, and seeing it made me realize how cold the house was with no heater. I shivered. I didn't want to re-enter the ghost room to fetch my jacket or a blanket. Instead, I went upstairs, climbed into Mom's bed, wrapped myself in her blankets and was asleep again in minutes.

The front door slammed, and I bolted upright, forgetting for a moment where I was. Pale blue light filtered through the windows.

"Girls?!" shouted Mom.

Footsteps pounded on the stairs and I rushed into the hallway.

"Sophia, good. Get your sister, pack up everything now, and get in the car."

"What's going on?" I asked.

"There's a social worker living up the street. We need to leave now."

I wasn't sure what a social worker was, but I'd heard the term used before Sapphira was taken away. Mom shoved me toward Eva's room, then headed into hers. I shook Eva until she woke up. "Hurry, get dressed and help me pack your things."

"Why?" she asked, rubbing her eyes.

"I don't know, just do it before Mom comes in here and yells at us."

Eva quickly threw her few clothes into the bag, followed by her dolls. I zipped it up for her and sent her downstairs with it.

I rushed to my room. Having never unpacked my clothes, I just punched them down, zipped up the suitcase, grabbed Wooby and headed downstairs. I gave Edgar my bag and got into the truck next to Eva, who sat in the middle, staring off into space.

We had changed vehicles so often I didn't pay attention to what it looked like, but I knew it was new. As long as I could sleep, what did it matter?

Another road trip, another new vehicle, another new place to live. Would we ever go back home?

This drive was the longest we'd taken since the trip from the farmhouse to the campsite with alligators. We left the ghost house as the sun came up and reached our new destination as the sun sank behind the horizon.

A maze of junk, old broken-down cars, and farm animals littered the front lawn of the small, ugly house we stopped in front of. The house had blue wooden siding, but the paint was peeling all over, making it look old and rundown. Behind the house, the junk, and the broken-down vehicles stood a barn. It had been red once, but there, too, the paint had peeled and faded. In front of where we parked was a clear pathway to the front door of the house.

As we climbed out of the truck, the stench of rotting food and engine oil met my nose.

We followed Edgar to the door, and as he knocked the sound of dogs barking greeted us.

"Shut up!" yelled a rough voice. The dogs didn't listen, and added to their noise came the sound of a horrible, hacking, loogie-making cough. Hearing it made me want to dry-heave. Gross.

A short, round woman opened the door, her breathing heavy and gurgled. Coughing again, she spit into a small can she held in her hand. My stomach felt queasy.

"Girls, this is my mom, Sally," said Edgar. "Your grandma."

And I thought things couldn't get any worse. *Note to self, things can always get worse.* "Nice to meet you," I said, plastering a fake smile on my face.

"Girls, give your new grandma a hug," said Mom, shoving us toward the woman.

Her short, silver hair stuck up in random places on her head. Old, worn slippers covered her feet. She wore a white, oversized muumuu with faded orange flowers and stains all over it, and she stunk of body odor. So it was a relief when she patted us both on the shoulder instead of drawing us in for a hug.

Two scruffy terriers stood behind her and yipped at us. She hacked up another loogie and spit into the can, apparently still recovering from her coughing fit. Sally nodded at us, then stepped back so we could enter. The stench of animal pee met my nose, and I recoiled, but Mom pushed me forward. We stood inside the dining room. The kitchen was on the left. Piles of dirty dishes lined the dingy white counters, and two cats nibbled wet cat food from paper plates. To the right lay a small living room, with a brown couch and a rocking chair. In front of these was a small, square TV, sitting atop a desk. The walls were painted wood. Not a single clean surface could be seen in any of the rooms. Newspapers, books, clothing, and knickknacks covered everything except the desk the TV was on.

"You guys can stay in the attic," she rasped, and pointed to a set of stairs on the other end of the living room.

"This place smells, Mom," whispered Eva as we carried our things up the narrow staircase.

"Shh, that's not a nice thing to say. Besides, you'll get used to it after a while."

The attic reminded me of the farmhouse, the walls sloping in to make a triangle. Two cots were stacked on top of each other under a small window. It was dark up here and full of dusty boxes. They had sheets, but I decided it would be safer to use our sleeping bags.

"How long are we going to stay here?" I asked.

"Not too long," said Mom. "Edgar has been talking with his contacts and we may have a more permanent place to stay soon."

Edgar, Mom, and Sally sat in the living room and talked for most of the evening. Eva and I explored outside a little, but there was nowhere to play or get away from the odors, so we tried to entertain ourselves with the toys we brought.

That night, when mom turned the light out, I tucked my head into the sleeping bag and squeezed my eyes shut. I imagined thousands of bugs crawling out from the walls, crawling in our ears, noses, and mouths, and suffocating us. Scooting further down into my sleeping bag, I tucked the open end under my head, but it was hot and hard to breathe. I forced myself to think of nice things so I could sleep.

The following day, Mom came with us as Eva and I explored outside. We weren't allowed to get into any of the cars, because it wasn't safe, but we walked around, peering in the windows of each vehicle and coming up with fun things we could build with all the junk lying around.

"What the heck is that?" asked Eva, pointing to a small creature that ambled along between rows of garbage.

Mom looked over and laughed. "That's an armadillo. Don't get too close to it. As a matter of fact, we should walk away and leave it alone."

The animal headed our direction and I watched it a moment longer, wondering if he had made his home here, or if he was a pet.

There was a yellow lab who mostly lived outside. I named him Blue. He followed me around everywhere, like I was his best friend. He snuggled up to me and let me pet him whenever I wanted. Eva wanted to pet him but was afraid.

"Don't be afraid, Eva, just pet him. He's not like the other dogs here, he's nice," I said.

Eva came close and reached her hand out to pet him. Blue bared his teeth and, before I could do anything about it, bit her hand.

Eva immediately started screaming and crying.

"Bad dog!" yelled Mom, and she picked up Eva and carried her inside.

"Blue, why would you do that? We can't be friends anymore if you're going to bite my sister," I said and went inside to check on my little sister.

Eva had calmed down, and I was relieved to see Blue hadn't broken the skin. There were only red, raised scratches on the back of her hand.

The next morning, I discovered Mom and Edgar had left us alone with the old woman. She sat in the rocking chair watching television, and I sat on the end of the couch nearest her. I'd never seen anyone watch TV this early in the day before. The images were black and white. I'd thought only my Grandma Joy, Mom's mom, still had a black-and-white TV.

"Morning," said Sally, holding the can she'd spit into yesterday in one hand and the television remote in the other.

"Good morning." I stared at the can, hoping she wouldn't have another coughing fit.

"Cereal is in the cupboard if you're hungry."

"Thank you." I stood to head to the kitchen and saw Eva standing behind the couch.

"Will you get me some cereal, too? I want to play with the cats when we're done eating," Eva said as we walked to the kitchen.

I nodded and found the cereal. Unable to find any clean dishes, I washed two bowls and spoons and made our breakfast. Finding a small section of uncluttered table, we set our bowls down and cleaned off two chairs.

"Where's Mom?" Eva asked.

"I don't know, they were gone when I got up."

Sally gave a long-gurgled cough and spit into the can. I put my spoon down and pushed the bowl away from me, too grossed out to eat now. A cat immediately jumped up on the table and lapped the milk.

"We need to ask about taking a shower," I said to Eva.

She nodded, milk dripping down her chin. Since I couldn't eat, I walked back to the living room.

"Sally, do you mind if we take a shower? We stink," I said, trying to be funny.

"There's a closet in the bathroom. You'll find everything you need in there," said Sally.

Not even a giggle. This lady is going to be tough to crack.

In the bathroom, I opened the closet and found the shelves lined with a lifetime supply of shampoo, conditioner, and body wash. I was also pleased to find clean towels, probably the only clean thing in this house.

Carrying a towel to Eva, who was about to pour a second bowl of cereal, I said, "I'm taking a shower while you eat."

She didn't respond. I could tell she was focused on not spilling cereal everywhere, so I walked away.

Never had being clean felt so good. I washed my hair twice and scrubbed at my fingers and toes with a washcloth until they were pink again. When I got out, Eva decided she wanted to take a bubble bath instead of a shower, and I filled the tub for her.

Sally didn't seem too bothered by us. She stared at the TV all day and spit into her can. When Eva got bored, she watched shows with Sally. Sometimes, I would too, but everything she watched was boring, so I mostly wandered around the house looking at all the junk.

The knickknacks all had chips, or the colors had faded, and books had pages torn out. Nothing here looked well taken care of. I found one interesting item in the attic, and that was the smallest guitar I'd ever seen. The wood was scratched, but the strings were okay. It had a faded blue and red design painted on it that looked like waves and a surfboard. *Mom would love this,* I thought. I took it upstairs to play with it.

Mom and Edgar didn't return that day. When I woke up the following morning and they still weren't back, I worried, thinking of Mom's illness at the farmhouse and imagining us being stuck here. We would slowly starve to death. I looked at Eva. Well, *I* would starve to death anyway, and then Eva would grow up in this filth.

Chapter 22

Around noon of our second day alone with Edgar's mom, I heard a car pull up outside and ran to the window.

"Mom!"

Finally. *Wait, what happened to the truck?* The passenger-side headlight dangled from its socket, and the side was scratched and dented.

"What happened?" I asked, running outside.

"A fox ran into the road, I swerved to miss it and crashed into the barrier," said Edgar.

"We almost drove right off a cliff," Mom said. "I couldn't get out of the truck because we were so close to the edge."

"Then the car wouldn't run, so we had to tinker with it. That's why we didn't get back last night," Edgar added.

"It was quite an adventure," said Mom, and they both laughed.

I clenched my fists. "That's not funny, Mom. What if you had died and left me and Eva here?"

"Well we didn't, so you don't need to worry about it, Sophia. Now, what happened while we were gone?"

"I have something cool to show you. It's in our room," I said.

"Cool, baby, give us a bit to get settled in, and you can show me," Mom said.

I sat at the table, waiting patiently for Mom to get settled, but instead she started doing the dishes. Instead of watching, I decided to help her and dry them. We talked about the past few days and what we had found during our exploration of the house. Mom didn't say much but listened. I was okay with that. Spending time with her was all I needed.

Cleaning the kitchen and dining area took all day, and when it was dark, Mom took us upstairs to get changed into pajamas.

"What was it you wanted to show me, Sophia?"

"This little itty-bitty guitar I found," I said, pulling it from under my cot. I started strumming the strings.

Mom laughed. "That's awesome. Tomorrow we can play with it for a while, but now it's bedtime and I'm exhausted." She tucked us in, gave us kisses, and went back downstairs.

In the middle of the night I woke up, my right ear throbbing. The whole right side of my head and neck felt hot. I considered the possibility of a bug eating its way through my skull and brain, but I'd had ear infections before, and that's what this felt like.

"Mom!" I cried out.

"What's the matter, baby?" came her sleepy voice.

"My ear hurts really bad."

Shuffling and grunting noises sounded nearby, and then the light turned on. Mom sat next to me and tilted my head so she could see into my ear.

"I'll see if I can find medicine for you," she said, grunting as she got to her feet.

Hugging Wooby tight, I cried; the pain seemed to get worse with the cold air touching it.

Mom came back holding a blow dryer. "I can't find a heating pad, so we'll have to use this. Hold it up to your ear while I finish warming oil and garlic on the stove."

The sound of the hair dryer woke Eva. I expected her to whine about not being able to sleep, but she surprised me. Not one complaint left her mouth, she helped me hold the dryer and helped Mom with the drops.

Every couple of hours I used the hair dryer and Mom added garlic oil drops and half a cotton ball in both ears. By the time the sun rose, the pain had lessened a little.

"Are you okay, Sophia?" asked Eva, when Mom left to make more garlic oil.

"Yeah, I think so. Thanks for helping me."

"It looked like it hurt a lot."

"Yeah, it sucks. I think it's from all the dirt and germs in this house and the last one," I said.

Eva glanced at the mess surrounding us and made a face as if just noticing the filth. "Yeah, this place is pretty dirty, now that you mention it."

Mom sat down next to me again. "How are you feeling, baby?"

"It still hurts a little, but it's a lot better," I said, scooting over to her and placing my head in her lap.

She stroked my hair. "Good. Edgar has to leave for a few days. Eva, do you think you can continue helping me put drops in Sophia's ears if she needs it?"

"Yeah, but where is Edgar going?" asked Eva.

"He's heading to a friend's house back east. We may have a good house to stay at for the winter."

"Anything would be better than this place," I said, holding my ear.

"I know. While Edgar is gone, I want to try to clean this place up a little bit to help Sally. That's why I'll need your help with these drops, Eva."

"Okay, Mommy." Eva grabbed some of her dolls and settled in next to me.

Mom paid more attention to us than she had this entire trip while Edgar was gone. She came up every hour or so to check on me and see if Eva was putting the drops in my ears the right way. I forgave her for making light of the accident they'd been in.

After two days, the pain in my ear was gone, but Mom still wanted me to keep cotton balls in my ears at night and when I took a shower.

We tried to play with the dogs, but they growled at us or ran away, so we left them alone. The cats let us pet them and were cute, but they didn't play games or do much of anything other than sleep.

Sometimes I thought about looking for tools and going outside to mess around with the junk cars, but I never found any tools. When I told Sally about my plan, she said it was too dangerous to tinker with old cars without knowing what I was doing. She also said the dogs might think I was trying to steal something and attack me. I didn't believe her. I figured she just didn't want us in the vehicle junkyard.

We watched a lot of TV because it passed the time. Sometimes Sally would put cartoons on, but most of the time she kept her game shows or soap operas on. When that got boring, we played with our toys, but we played the same games over and over until they weren't fun anymore.

One afternoon, I sat next to Mom and Sally as they watched *Wheel of Fortune*. I had a question for Sally, but apparently the only acceptable time to have a conversation was during a commercial.

"Do you like being a grandma?" I asked when one finally came on.

Sally shrugged. "I'm not used to having kids around, but I guess it's all right."

"Do you have any other grandkids?"

She shook her head, "No." Talking made her cough, so she didn't ever say much. She started hacking now, so I stared at my hands resting in my lap and tried to think of something that would distract me from the disgusting noise.

Spitting into her can and taking deep, gurgling breaths, she said, "Never smoke."

"Is that why you cough?"

She nodded.

"Are you sick?"

"I'm dying, slowly," she rasped through gurgled breaths.

"But I haven't seen you smoke since we've been here. Won't you get better?"

"No. Some sicknesses you don't get better from."

172

I looked around at the messy house. Mom had tried to clean it up some, and it smelled and looked better, but there was nowhere to put all the garbage, except outside with the other junk piles. How sad it would be to die all alone in a place like this. Maybe that's why Mom wanted to help her.

"Sorry," I said quietly.

Sally reached over and squeezed my arm and we continued watching her show in silence.

That evening, Sally made dinner. It was the most I'd seen her move since we'd been there.

"I hope you girls like grilled cheese sandwiches," rasped Sally.

Eva jumped up and down and clapped her hands. "I do, I do, I do!"

Sally placed two on a napkin and carried them to the living room. Mom, Eva and I stayed in the kitchen. The cheese was white instead of yellow, but other than that it looked like a grilled cheese sandwich. I took a bite then immediately spit it out. It tasted like burned sour milk.

"I can't eat this," I said to Mom.

Eva took a big bite of hers and gagged. The lump of half-chewed sandwich fell on the floor.

"Quit being dramatic, girls. It can't be that bad." Mom took a bite of hers, made a face and spit it back out. "Okay, maybe it is that bad. I think this is goat cheese." She took our sandwiches, opened the window and tossed them out. "Let the dogs eat them."

All three of us gathered around the window and watched as the dogs sniffed the food. When they walked away without touching the sandwiches, we all laughed.

Mom looked in the fridge for something else we could eat, found some normal cheese, and made us each a real grilled cheese sandwich. We sat at the kitchen table, eating and chatting.

Sally shuffled in and threw her napkin in the garbage can. "Looks like one of my cats had kittens early today," she said. "You girls can take a look at them later if you want."

The next day, Eva and I entertained ourselves for about an hour by watching the kittens. Sally had put a towel in the bottom of a cardboard box by the stairs for them. We wanted to hold them, but if we got too close, mama cat would hiss, and Sally said if we touched them too soon, their mom would reject them. We quickly got bored and left them alone.

Each day seemed to get longer and longer. It had been more than a week since Edgar left, and he still wasn't back. I was ready to leave this place. I threw myself on the couch to watch TV with Sally, but I couldn't focus on the show. I thought about my family back home and wondered if they were looking for us. Eva hadn't recognized her dad. Was it possible our family had forgotten about us?

The more I thought about our family back home, the sadder I got, and soon, tears rolled down my cheeks. Mom was cleaning in the kitchen and Eva was at the table playing with one of the cats, so they wouldn't see me cry. I didn't want them to. Sally sat nearby, engrossed in her show, so I laid down on the couch and buried by face in the cushions, trying to cry quietly so she wouldn't notice. The more I cried, the better I felt. Wooby was crumpled in the corner of the couch nearest my head. I grabbed it and pulled it to my chest. Eventually I fell fast asleep.

Chapter 23

4 Months Before The FBI Standoff

Edgar returned four days later. "We're leaving here and heading to a new place tomorrow morning," he told us.

Finally. I hadn't been so excited to leave a place since the bus.

"Where are we going?" asked Eva.

"Wisconsin, to stay with friends of Jack. Their names are Jamie and Chris."

"That's wonderful," Mom said. "I cleaned the house a little for your mom. It's the least I could do for her hospitality."

"Thanks, hun. Girls, get your things together tonight so we can load up and be on the road early."

Before it turned thoroughly disgusting, our last full day at Sally's was just as boring as ever. That night, Sally ordered a pizza, and for once my stomach was full.

"When we get to our destination, I'll call you. The less you know, the better," Edgar told his mom.

"I'll be fine, son."

"Just in case, I'll give you a phone number so you can reach me if you need to," he said through a mouth full of food.

As much as I hated to admit it, I liked Edgar a little more after watching him interact with his mom. Sure, he had strange friends, and weird beliefs, but mostly he was a nice person. And after the one time he spanked Eva, he'd never hit any of us again. Yelled, yes, but never hit.

"Mom, what is that cat doing?" asked Eva.

The kittens had found their way out from behind the boxes, and the mama cat licked and chewed on one of their bellies.

"Eating the umbilical cord of her baby."

"What's an umbiblical cord?" asked Eva.

"When the babies were inside the mama cat, they got food from the cords."

"Ew, and she's eating it? That's disgusting."

I agreed and turned my attention back to the television.

A few minutes later, the cat sat on the floor in front of us making a strange coughing noise, her body convulsing. After a few seconds of this, the cat threw up slimy, green goo all over Mom's new white shoes.

"Ew, that's worse than horse poop!" yelled Eva, hiding her face in her hands.

Everyone laughed except me. I was too busy trying to keep down my pizza.

"Help me clean it up, Sophia," said Mom.

"Why me?" I swallowed hard several times.

"Because I have to clean off my shoes, Edgar's been driving all day, Sally is sick, and Eva is too young."

"There's a small hand brush and dustpan in the kitchen somewhere," said Sally.

I shook my head. "No, I can't. I will throw up everywhere."

You would have thought I just told them the funniest joke they'd ever heard. I kept swallowing until I was sure I wouldn't puke.

"Are you okay, Sophia?" asked Eva, putting her hand on my arm.

It wasn't fair that my little sister, who got freaked out by everything, had no trouble keeping her food down.

The adults pulled themselves together and stopped laughing. "Come on, Soph, let's clean this up." Mom slapped my leg as she stood.

I wasn't dry-heaving anymore, so maybe I would be all right. I found the items Sally mentioned and returned. The green goop smelled awful, so I tried to only breathe through my mouth. I bent down and attempted to sweep the wet pile off Mom's shoes into the dustpan.

The vomit stuck to the brush and when I pulled it away; it was stringy. I dry-heaved, dropped the dustpan and brush, and turned away, swallowing hard several times so I wouldn't throw up.

Mom laughed so hard she was bent over, almost on the floor, with tears streaming down her cheeks.

"I … can't …" I gasped. Soon, I had control of my stomach again, but made the mistake of breathing through my nose. The rancid stench of vomit made me heave again. "Nope, I can't do it."

"It's okay, Sophia, go over there and sit down." Mom continued laughing for several minutes, but managed to carry her shoes to the kitchen and rinse them off in the sink.

"Girls, it's time for bed. Go get your jammies on," Edgar said.

The next morning, we packed our things into a different car than the one we'd arrived in. My stomach was in knots, and I couldn't eat breakfast. I wasn't sure if my stomach was still queasy from the evening before, or if it was the possibility of meeting up with Richard, Jack, and the others again that was making me feel this way.

I bunched Wooby into a ball to use as a pillow and tried to fall asleep. But for a long time I could only stare out the window and think about Sapphira. No matter how hard I tried to think about something else, my mind kept returning to my big sister being dragged away. Eventually, I slept, but when the car stopped I sat up, stretched, and peered out the window into the darkness. A huge house, big enough for the whole group from before, stood in front of us. My stomach did somersaults at the sight.

Sapphira being dragged away, Mom crying, and the police. Would they make me get married?

I tried to stuff down my fears in preparation to see the others again. I reminded myself of their rules and hoped my first meal with them wouldn't make me tired.

"Where are we?" asked Eva. She was ignored, and we climbed out of the car. Making out details of the house in the dark was difficult, but what I could see was amazing. Trees and bushes crowded the yard like a forest.

As we reached the door, a path appeared between the house and the bushes that looked like it wrapped around the side. That would be fun to explore. That is, if they allowed me to.

A tall, skinny woman in jeans and a long-sleeved plaid shirt opened the door. She had a small, black poodle in her arms that reminded me of Midnight, and her brown, curly hair bounced around her face when she spoke.

I didn't recognize her. Maybe this wasn't where the group lived, after all.

"Hey there! Welcome, come on in," the woman said, smiling.

She moved to let us pass through. There was a doorway to the right, down a short set of carpeted beige stairs. To the left were more of the same stairs, going up. A white wall lined the staircase, and at the top was a brown couch, which looked like leather, next to a black railing. The small space we stood in was apparently only used as an entrance. There were coat hangers on the wall, and a shelf for shoes.

"My name is Jamie. This is my husband, Chris," she said, gesturing to a man standing behind her, who smiled at us. "Please take your shoes off here."

Chris was the same height as Jamie. He had a buzz cut and huge arm muscles that made his shirt look too small for him.

Each of us slipped our shoes off and set them on the rack.

"Let me show you where you'll stay while you're here," Jamie said.

They led us down the stairs to the right of the front door, to the basement; the floor was concrete and the walls bare. A divider wall, which you could walk around if you wanted to, separated the room into two areas. A bunk bed stood on one side of the divider wall and another bed stood on the wall opposite the stairs.

"We haven't had a chance to get carpet in here, but it should be nice and cozy for you all. I'm sure you're tired, so we'll let you get settled. Tomorrow we can give you a tour of the place and help you unload your car," Jamie said, before going back upstairs.

Eva and I crawled onto the bottom bunk and Mom tucked us in, kissing each of us on the cheek.

"Goodnight, girls."

Relieved that this big, amazing house had none of those crazy people in it, I drifted off to sleep.

I woke before everyone else. There was nothing interesting to look at, so I got out of bed and paced the room. Could I go upstairs? My stomach growled, I was so hungry.

"Mom?" I whispered, tapping her arm. No response. "Mom," I said a little louder, shaking her.

"Go back to bed," she groaned and swatted at me with her hand.

My tummy growled again, and I sighed. If the rest of the community showed up here, I wouldn't know what the rules were until I broke them. Jamie seemed nice last night, so if going up there was against the rules, hopefully she wouldn't yell at me. I tried to be quiet so I could look around without being seen, but the stairs creaked. With each noise, I stopped to listen but heard nothing.

I tiptoed through the entrance and peeked around the other doorway that apparently led to the living room. All clear. When I was halfway through the living room, the scent of bacon reached my nose. The kitchen was in view, and I saw a movement. Slowly and quietly, I headed that way.

Jamie stood at the stove, cooking. "Are you hungry?" she asked without looking at me.

How did she know I was here? I didn't answer right away. Would she think I was selfish if I didn't wait for the rest of my family? "Yes, I am."

"Have a seat at the table, breakfast is almost ready," Jamie said, still not looking at me.

I nodded, took a seat at one of the solid wood chairs, stained a dark, rich brown to match the table, and watched her. Or rather, I watched her hands to see what she put in the food.

When she walked away from the food to grab a stack of plates, I glanced around at the kitchen. The floor was hardwood and the cabinets were white. The stove looked like an older model and had actual fire under the pans instead of coils.

Jamie loaded food onto two plates. Something about this lady made me want to like her. But then again, I'd liked other people too, and then bad things happened.

Now and then, Jamie would smile at me, but neither of us said anything. Placing a plate full of eggs and toast in front of me, she brought me a fork and set a jar of strawberry jam on the table. My mouth watered at the sight, but I waited for her to sit with her plate before I ate.

"How did you sleep?" asked Jamie.

"Good, thank you."

She took her first bite, then I picked up my fork, stabbed several chunks of egg and shoved them into my mouth. She had put salt and pepper on the eggs while cooking, and the flavors burst on my tongue. I took a large bite of the toast. Melted butter, yum. Jam would have been amazing, but I didn't want to stop eating.

Jamie watched me as I ate. I probably looked like someone who hadn't eaten in months, but I didn't care.

Cleaning my plate, I looked around, unsure what to do next.

"All done?" she asked.

Well, duh, there was no food left on my plate. Wait, was she asking if I wanted more? Children weren't allowed seconds in the community. Did this mean Jamie and Chris weren't part of the group, or did they consider me an adult?

"I am full, thank you." I got up, wanting to explore, but went back downstairs to see if the others were up yet.

Everyone was awake. Mom made up the beds and Eva sat on the floor playing with a doll.

"Morning," I said. "Mom, I like that lady upstairs. She's nice."

"Mmhmm." Mom seemed deep in thought, and I wondered if she really heard what I said. When she was done with our bed, I sat on it. For almost the first time on this journey, I had a full belly—and hope that we were with people who liked kids.

Chapter 24

When Mom and Eva went upstairs for breakfast, I followed. Jamie would tell Mom the rules.

Chris sat at the table eating. He smiled at us, and I wondered if he ever spoke.

"Help yourselves, there's plenty to go around," said Jamie. "Sophia, since you and I have already eaten, do you want to help me unload your things?"

"Sure." I followed her, and we carried the bags and toys in and down to the basement.

"Now, from the looks of it, none of you have had a proper shower in a while, which means your clothes could probably use a wash, too. Let's grab all of them and take them up to the laundry room, okay?"

"Okay." I unzipped my bag and Eva's, took out the clothes, and piled them on the floor. The treasures I'd collected were in my bag. I kept the flap down so Jamie wouldn't see them. As I zipped it closed, the shotgun shells rolled around and clinked together.

Jamie looked in my direction at the noise. I shoved the bag under the bunk bed and zipped up Eva's. Then, we both grabbed a armful of clothes and headed upstairs.

She led me through the kitchen to a small porch area with a washer and dryer on one wall. Several small windows lined the opposite wall, and a clothesline hung across the center of the room.

Dumping our loads onto the floor, Jamie said, "Thanks for your help, I'll take care of the rest."

I nodded and headed back to the kitchen. Chris stood at the sink washing dishes, and Mom and Eva sat at the table looking out the big window at the backyard. I joined them and waited for someone to tell us what to do.

Jamie joined us a few minutes later. "Well, are we ready for a tour of the house?"

I smiled. Now we would hear the rules for sure.

"Your house is lovely," said Mom.

"Thank you," said Jamie.

"What is your dog's name?" asked Eva. The little dog sat on Chris' feet as he dried the last of the dishes.

"That's Toots," said Chris.

So he did speak.

"Toots? That's a funny name. Does your dog fart a lot?" asked Eva.

Everyone laughed.

"No, it's short for Tootsie Roll, like the candy," said Chris.

Jamie took us into every room on the main floor. Besides the living room, kitchen, and laundry room, there was a bathroom with a really big tub that I couldn't wait to use, and Jamie and Chris's bedroom. The kitchen had a balcony off one side, but it needed repairs, so we couldn't walk on it.

After the house tour, she took us out back. Their backyard was amazing. Like the front, there were trees and bushes everywhere. There was also a trampoline, and Jamie said we could play on it whenever we wanted to, as long as it wasn't wet.

"Okay, girls, I'm going to show you something else we have back here. I need you to promise me you won't use it unless you have permission and there's an adult who can watch you."

Eva and I nodded, both excited to see what it was.

Jamie walked backwards a few steps, then crooked her finger at us and smiled. When we were near her, she pointed to a tree a few feet away. Wooden planks, nailed to the trunk, went all the way up and disappeared into the leaves.

"Go on, climb up and see what you find."

I ran to the tree and climbed.

"Wait for me," said Eva.

Ignoring her, I climbed as fast as possible. When my head reached the spot where the leaves covered the wood planks, I stopped for a moment, looking down. It was high, and I couldn't help but giggle. A trap door appeared above me. I pulled on it until it opened, then climbed the last few planks and found myself in the most amazing tree house I'd ever seen.

Eva joined me a moment later, and we explored every inch together.

The little house was closed in on all sides, with a roof and everything, and there were windows. Actual panes of glass, at least two on each wall. Several trees stood close to this one, hiding it from view. Many of the leaves had fallen off the tree, but there were still enough to make it hard to see anything on the ground. I tried to imagine it in the summer, when it would be surrounded by green leaves. It would make the perfect place to hide.

"This is awesome!" said Eva.

When we climbed down again, Jamie and Mom were waiting for us.

"What did you think?" asked Jamie.

"That is the coolest tree house in the history of all the tree houses, ever!" said Eva.

"I'm glad you like it. Just remember, you can only go up there if an adult is around. Now, I need to head back inside. I've got some things to do today. Feel free to stay outside and play. Tonight, we'll see what we can do about all the dirt you two have collected."

That's it? No rules about school, or prayer, or anything?

"Trampoline?" Eva asked me hopefully.

"Race you!" I answered and took off. Eva ran too, but I beat her easily and climbed on the trampoline.

"That's not fair, you didn't give me a head start," she whined, looking up at me from the ground.

"You didn't ask for one," I smirked, bouncing.

After dinner that evening, Jamie took us to the bathroom and filled the tub with warm water. "Here is a washcloth for each of you, and some soap. I'll come back in a little while to check on you."

Eva and I sat in the tub for a long time, enjoying the warm water and splashing each other.

Jamie checked on us a couple of times and brought our clean clothes, setting them on the counter nearby. Clean jammies made me feel happy.

"Goodness, you girls were dirty. That tub used to be white," said Jamie, as the three of us joined the others in the living room.

Staring at the floor, I waited to hear what our punishment would be for not thinking to clean the tub when we got out, but Jamie only laughed.

"I won't worry about cleaning it until Edgar takes his shower. That man probably has more dirt on him than both girls combined."

Everyone laughed, and I relaxed a little.

"Yeah, I guess that means it's my turn. I'll clean it when I'm done if you show me where the cleaner is." Edgar stretched and stood up.

"Well, I won't turn down an offer like that," said Jamie, following him out of the room.

"Girls, bedtime. One of you can sleep on the top bunk tonight," said Mom.

"I want the top," said Eva.

"There isn't a bar to keep you from falling off the side," I said.

"I won't fall off, I'm a big girl."

"You will fall off."

"I won't!"

"Stop, let your sister sleep on the top if she wants to," said Mom.

Rolling my eyes as we headed downstairs, I whispered, "You're going to fall off," when we were out of earshot from Mom.

Eva climbed up to the top bunk, then stuck her tongue out at me before crawling under her covers.

I snuggled under my blankets on the lower bunk. This place was amazing. Jamie and Chris were so nice, and they had plenty of food.

When we'd been at the campground by the lake, I could've stayed there forever, but now I knew better. If I couldn't go back home, if I had to choose from all the places we'd stayed at, I'd choose here.

As I drifted to sleep, peace enveloped me. It was the first time I'd felt this way since I'd accidently hanged myself a few years ago.

Something fell onto my mattress and I sat bolt upright, my heart pounding. Eva was crying.

Reaching out my hand to touch the large lump next to me, to make sure it was really her, I whispered, "Eva?"

"I fell off the top bunk," she whimpered.

I laughed.

"Shut up, it's not funny."

I wrapped my arms around her. "You're all right. At least you landed on the bed instead of the concrete floor."

After a few minutes, she calmed down. "Can I sleep with you?" she asked.

"Sure." We rearranged the blankets so we would both have enough, then I kissed her forehead. Soon, we were both sound asleep.

Let's stop for today," said Stacy. "Andy is waiting for me so we can go home."

I glanced at the clock and was surprised to find we'd been talking for almost three hours.

"Yeah, I can't believe we went way over our time." I gathered my things, we set another time to meet next week, and I left.

I sat in my car and turned it on but stayed in the parking lot for a while, thinking about everything I'd shared with Stacy so far. Except for the few comments she made when I told her about accidentally hanging myself, Stacy mostly just listened. I'd thought a lot about what she said about the man with the fire eyes being Jesus. The only thing I knew about Jesus is that he was supposed to be the brother of Lucifer. I turned the radio on and scanned the channels for something to listen to on my drive home.

What did I really know about God? Only what I'd been taught. Stacy, in her way, was trying to teach me, too, but how could I believe what anyone said unless I investigated things for myself?

"Have you given your heart to Jesus yet?" said a voice on the radio. I stopped scanning channels and listened.

Chapter 25

I sat down for my third session with Stacy on the now-familiar couch in her office, and grabbed a pillow for my lap so I could lean forward and rest my elbows on it.

"How have you been this past week?" asked Stacy.

"I'm struggling. My roommates keep saying they don't even know who I am anymore and I'm different, and I don't know what to think about that. I don't feel any different, I haven't even made up my mind about what I think about all this God stuff."

"Have you been praying like I suggested?"

"Yes, but it still feels weird, like I'm talking to myself."

Stacy smiled, "I think your roommates are sensing that. Being willing to open yourself up to the idea that God is real, he loves you, and wants to heal you, gives God an opening to begin the healing process. Even if you don't see it right now, or things don't look like they're getting any better, your willingness to open up your heart, even just a little, is enough for God to do some amazing things."

"I see." On my drive home from work I'd been listening to a Pastor Kayzik on a local radio station. He'd said something the other day about how God changes people from the inside out and other people would be able to see it.

"Do you have any questions before you continue with your story?" asked Stacy.

"If God changes me, will I still ... be me?"

"Of course. God created you to be you, but, in the case of your story, sin has had its effect on your life through trauma. All God wants to do is help you heal from that trauma so you can be the best version of you."

"That makes sense." I relaxed a little but decided I still needed to do more research before making up my mind.

"Any other questions or concerns?" asked Stacy.

"Not right now." Besides listening to the pastor on the radio, my evenings were spent reading the Bible to search for answers. So yes, I had questions I could ask Stacy, but I wanted to keep researching on my own. If, at the end of our sessions, her answers lined up with what I was learning, I might put some faith in this Christianity stuff.

"Great, we stopped after Eva fell off the top bunk in this new house with the militia people," said Stacy.

"Right. It was impossible to be bored there. One day, Chris brought out two slingshots and showed us how to use them."

"Remember, aim away from the house, cars, people, and animals, unless it's a jackrabbit. Everything else is fair game," said Chris.

He gave us each a small leather bag for collecting ammo, and we took off to find some small rocks.

"Let's pretend we're cavemen and these are the only weapons we have to hunt for food," I said to Eva.

"But we're not allowed to shoot at animals except the rabbits, and I don't want to hurt a rabbit."

"That's why we pretend. The bushes can be animals, and the big boulders can be our enemies."

"Okay, but I want to be the princess cave girl," said Eva.

"There's no such thing," I said, rolling my eyes.

"Yes, huh, princesses are real."

"Yeah, but cave people didn't have princesses."

"How do you know?" asked Eva.

"I just do, now let's play."

"No, I want to be a princess." Eva crossed her arms and scowled.

"Fine, be a princess, but you still have to fight, I won't rescue you," I said.

"Fine."

We chased and shot down invisible bad guys until Jamie called us in for lunch: macaroni and cheese with hot dogs. Real kid food. It tasted amazing.

"What have you been playing out there?" asked Jamie.

"Cavemen. I was a princess cave girl, but I knew how to fight and didn't need rescuing," said Eva.

"Being able to defend yourself seems like a great skill for a princess," said Jamie.

"The slingshots are a lot of fun," I said.

"I'm glad you like them, Sophia."

"Can I go in the tree house after lunch?"

Jamie smiled, "I don't see why not. I'll be working in the greenhouse and can keep an eye on the two of you."

Coming from Stewart or Richard, that sentence would have terrified me, but it sounded friendly coming from Jamie.

"Thank you."

"Where's my mom?" asked Eva.

"Your mom and Edgar are searching for work," said Jamie.

"Oh, okay."

I loved that Jamie answered our questions. "Do you want help cleaning up?" I asked.

"That would be lovely, thank you. I'll wash, you dry."

Following her over to the sink, I waited for the first dish.

"So, I understand your family has been on quite the journey."

"Yeah."

"How have you liked the trip so far?" asked Jamie.

I shrugged. "It's been okay. Some places were fun, and others I was glad to leave."

Jamie laughed. "That seems to be how life goes, doesn't it?"

I nodded.

"When I was about your age, my family took me on a road trip. Not as long as the one you've been on, but we drove for days, visiting national parks along the way. One place we stopped for the night had a big, open area; I was so excited to get out of the car and run around. It was so hot outside I left my shoes in the car. Before I realized the field was a bunch of weeds with sharp edges that scratched up my feet, I was in the center of it. I froze and begged my parents to bring me my shoes or carry me to the car." Jamie shook her head. "It was awful. My feet hurt so bad the rest of the night I couldn't run around and play like I'd planned. I remember little else from that trip, except we went to the beach. That part was fun."

I looked at her, horrified, imagining plants with razor-blade leaves and bloodied feet. "Did your parents save you, or make you run back?"

Jamie stopped washing the pan in her hands and looked at me. She smiled, but it seemed like a sad smile. "My dad rescued me. He picked me up and carried me over his shoulder like a sack of potatoes."

It was difficult imagining Jamie that small. "Do you still talk to your dad?"

"No sweetie, the good Lord took him home several years ago."

"I'm sorry," I said quietly.

"It's quite all right. He was a good dad and I will cherish the memories." She smiled, wrapped her arms around my shoulders and squeezed them. "Okay, we're all done. Thanks again for your help."

We walked out back, Jamie's arm still around my shoulders. She gave me one last squeeze before releasing me. "I'll be over here if you need me. Be careful climbing up the ladder."

She brushed my hair from my face and rubbed my cheek with her thumb, probably trying to remove dirt. "Have fun."

I smiled and ran to the tree, climbing as fast as I could. There were a lot of hidden places to store treasure, but they were all empty. For a while, I sat on the worn planks with the windows propped open, listening to the breeze, birds, and the sound of Jamie talking below to Eva, who had decided to help Jamie in the green house.

I felt safe up here. Safe and invisible.

"Sophia? It's time to come down, now."

I thought about ignoring her until someone climbed up to get me, but Jamie was nice, so I obeyed.

Once I reached the ground again, Jamie waited for me by the back door. When I walked through it, she wrapped her arm around my shoulder and hugged me to her.

"How would you like to help me make dinner tonight?"

I shrugged, "Sure. I'm not a very good cook, though."

"That's okay, I'll teach you."

Mom, Edgar, and Chris were in the living room, talking, but stopped and stared at me when we walked in.

"Sophia is going to help make dinner tonight." Jamie guided me to the kitchen, away from the others. I glanced over my shoulder when she dropped her arm. They were still staring, and Edgar nodded his head slowly.

Jamie handed me a head of lettuce, got out a chopping board and a knife, then showed me how to chop the lettuce for a salad. My hands were clumsy with the task. She watched for a moment, then gathered other food items from the fridge and pantry.

The others talked in low voices. Listening was out of the question. I was too busy trying not to cut my fingers off with the big knife.

Scooping the lettuce from the cutting board into a bowl, I heard Edgar say, "Yeah, we should teach her to shoot."

The promise he made me at the campsite returned to my mind, and a ball of excited butterflies fluttered in my stomach.

Three days passed and no one had said anything to me about learning to shoot a gun. Hope dampened. But on the fourth day, Edgar followed Chris to the trampoline where Eva and I were playing.

"Will you please join us, Sophia?" asked Chris.

I stopped jumping and looked at Chris's smiling face. He was a quiet person, never saying much, but he always wore a friendly smile.

Climbing down, I followed them to the other side of the backyard. We reached a small locked shed. Chris unlocked it, then pulled out a big gun and held it in front of me.

"This is a BB gun, and we're going to teach you how to shoot it," he said.

A grin spread across my face as I looked from one man to the other.

"Okay, first things first. Gun safety. Unless you intend to shoot someone, never point a gun at people. Keep the barrel in the air, or pointed at the ground. Got it?" asked Chris.

"Got it."

Chris kneeled next to me and turned the gun on its side. "This is the safety. Whenever you aren't using the gun, the safety should be on." He brought the gun to his shoulder. "Whenever you're holding the gun, rest your finger on the side, not on the trigger. The only time your finger should be on the trigger is when you're ready to shoot. Got that so far? Any questions?"

"Yes. No questions, yet," I said.

"Great," he handed me the gun.

I took it, carefully pointing the barrel toward the ground, like he'd told me.

"Now wait a minute—where is that barrel pointing?" asked Edgar.

Glancing up at him, then down at the barrel, I swung the gun away from his feet.

"Good girl," said Chris. "Let's head to the front of the house. We set up targets for you to shoot at."

He led me around to the secret pathway between the house and bushes, and then the trees and bushes parted, revealing a big shooting range. I was amazed. It all looked so natural, but the plants had been placed strategically to hide this place. Cool!

He showed me how to aim, and after an hour, I was hitting most of the soda cans they'd lined up on a log.

"Great job. We'll stop for today. Tomorrow I'll teach you how to shoot sitting, kneeling, and lying down."

"This is fun, thanks for teaching me." I handed the gun back to Chris.

"Whoa, now, we're done shooting, but there is still one thing we have to do with that gun."

Frowning, I checked that the safety was on—it was—then looked back at Chris.

"We have to clean it."

We sat down on the log that had held the soda cans, and he showed me how to open the gun and clean out the barrel. After spraying something called solvent on a piece of cotton, he told me to make sure it was the kind that wouldn't catch on fire; then he showed me how to use a long string with a loop on the end to pull the wet cotton through the barrel.

I used three cotton pads before it came out clean.

"Tomorrow, you get to do the whole process by yourself," Chris said.

"How was it?" asked Jamie when we got back to the house.

"Fun! I can't wait to shoot again tomorrow."

"I'll tell you what, Jamie, this girl is a fast learner," Chris said.

"I want to learn to shoot, too," said Eva.

"Sorry, kiddo, you're too young, but when you're older we'll teach you, okay?"

"Okay, you promise, Chris?"

"I pinkie-swear," said Chris, holding his little finger out to her.

She hooked her own into his and smiled.

Before bed that night, I tucked her in. "Eva, when I'm allowed to take the gun out by myself, I promise to teach you how to shoot. Deal?"

"Do you really promise? Will you pinkie-promise like Chris did?"

"Yes, I pinkie-promise." I held out my little finger and she wrapped hers around mine, and we shook on it.

Every day that week, Chris and Edgar let me shoot the gun. Each day brought new things to learn, but we always started with safety.

On the second day, they taught me how to shoot sitting, lying down, crouched over, and standing sideways. My favorite was lying on the ground. I felt like a spy or a sharpshooter. I practiced all day, while they took turns observing and correcting when needed.

They also taught me how to use a scope. "If you're not careful, the gun could recoil back, causing the scope to give you a black eye," Chris explained.

I laughed at the thought; I was obviously a natural at this, and that would never happen to me.

By day three, I tired of shooting at cans. It was too easy. "Can I try something new now?"

"Well, you are catching on pretty fast. Are you ready to learn how to group your shots in the different positions we taught you?" asked Chris.

"Oh, yeah!"

They pulled out a cardboard cutout of a human that had little bullseyes on various body parts.

"If you hit a person at any of these points, it will take them down but won't kill them. Why do you think this is important to know?" asked Chris.

"Because killing people is bad?"

"No, sometimes killing people is necessary, like in war. The reason it's important is so you can interrogate them. Do you know what that means?"

I shook my head.

"That means to question someone. People in a lot of pain will always give information. Sometimes you might have to shoot them more than once, but eventually they'll cave."

"Why would I need to question someone? Couldn't I just call the police?"

Chris raised his eyebrows. "Sure, but police work for the government. People who work for the government only care about what they can get. Usually money. So, if someone breaks into a house, the robber might get away before the cops get there. They'll tell you they're still working on the case, but you'll have no proof and you'll never see your stuff again.

"If you shoot the person, the police will take him to the hospital to be patched up and send him on his way. On top of all that, you might get in trouble for shooting the guy. It's better to know how to protect yourself if needed. Never rely on cops or the government."

The more he talked, the redder his face got; he looked kind of scary that way, but what he said made sense. I hadn't been able to protect myself or my sisters since we left home. Maybe all this stuff they were teaching me would come in handy if we had to join the others again. I imagined Richard coming toward me with an angry scowl, holding the paddle, and me pointing a gun at him. No way would he dare hurt me or Eva again if that happened, of that I was sure.

The next day, there was a different cardboard cutout. It was a person again, but the bullseyes were in different places. That was the day they taught me where to shoot to kill. They also had a plastic deer and taught me the basics of hunting.

Carrying that gun around and learning to shoot it gave me confidence. Almost every day, I asked to take it out to practice, and unless it was snowing, they let me. After two weeks, they let me shoot targets by myself, so I grabbed Eva to teach her, like I promised. I showed her how to hold the gun, the rules about where to place your finger, the safety, and how to hold the gun when not in use. Then I showed her how to aim and let her practice on the targets until she got bored. I kept an eye out for any of the adults who might come over to check on me.

"Promise you won't tell anyone about this," I said, when Eva decided she was done.

"I won't."

"Good, because if they find out, we'll both get in trouble," I said.

"Do you think they'll spank us, like Richard did?"

"Probably." I didn't think Jamie or Chris would really spank us, but Eva would keep her mouth shut if she thought another dirty sock would get taped in her mouth.

Chapter 26

Christmas was less than a week away. As I had with my
birthday, I tried not to get my hopes up, which wasn't hard because I
kept thinking about Sapphira. Where was she? How would she be
celebrating Christmas, and who would she be celebrating with? This
strange life had so many ups, downs, and changes, it was impossible
to tell if we'd get Christmas, or if we'd move again before the
holiday.

Jamie and Chris seemed like people who would make sure we
got a Christmas, but they had some odd ideas. Their basement was
full of canned food from their garden. They had several storage
lockers filled with guns, and sometimes they said strange things that
reminded me of Stewart and the others, only it was all about the
government and not about religion.

Eva talked about Christmas nonstop. I tried to tell her not to
expect much, especially since no one had brought out decorations
and there was no talk about putting up a Christmas tree. But nothing
I said could convince her. According to her, Santa had strong enough
magic to find all the kids in the entire world.

A couple of days had passed since I'd asked if I could shoot the
gun. In fact, I hadn't been in the mood to do much of anything except
follow Jamie around the house, helping her with odd jobs. This
morning I peeled and cut pears while she canned them.

"Why did you stay inside and help me, instead of playing with
your sister?" she asked.

I shrugged. "I don't really want to play."

"Is everything okay? You've been down lately," said Jamie.

"I miss my big sister, Sapphira."

Jamie paused, and the tongs she used to pull jars out of the water bath trembled slightly. "I didn't know you had an older sister. Where is she?"

Another shrug. "A social worker took her away when we lived in the big brick house."

"I'm sorry to hear that." Jamie was silent for a few minutes and focused her attention on watching the jars in the pot. I continued cutting pears.

"Hey, there you are," said Edgar, walking into the kitchen. "Sophia, how would you like to go hunting tomorrow morning?"

"You want me to go hunting with you?"

Except for the fishing trip meant to distract us from learning about Sapphira's wedding and teaching me to shoot, Edgar had barely acknowledged my existence. Now he wanted to take me hunting?

"Yeah, you've been practicing with your gun for a while now, why not put those skills to use on a moving target?"

"Okay."

Edgar nodded and walked out of the room. Jamie smiled at me. "You'll have fun," said Jamie.

The next morning, Edgar woke me up before the sun shone through the windows. We ate a quick breakfast, then headed out, me with my BB gun, and Edgar with one of Chris' rifles. I followed him to the backyard past the tree house. Behind the property was a dirt road, which we followed past several fields. We finally cut through one of them to a wooded area. Edgar let me rest for a few minutes before we continued. It was still dark outside, but the moon shining on the snow made it easy to see.

"The deer have a fantastic sense of smell and great hearing, so we need to be quiet. If I motion for you to move in a certain direction; you need to listen, got it?" whispered Edgar.

I nodded. He handed me a pair of hunting earmuffs. "Put these on. This gun is loud. It's not much further now."

I obeyed, and we were off. Edgar kept close to the trees and I followed, making mental notes about how much quieter our footsteps were walking on wet leaves and not crunching through the white powder.

After a fifteen-minute walk, we came to a small wooden hut with two windows. The entrance didn't have a door, and there were no glass panes or coverings on the windows.

"Now we'll wait and see if any deer come our way," whispered Edgar.

Inside the small hut stood two small stumps of wood, which we used as chairs. I leaned my BB gun on the wall next to me. Edgar pulled a thermos out of a bag he carried, and poured a hot liquid into the lid that also served as a cup, and handed it to me. Hot chocolate.

Slowly sipping the drink, I alternately stared out the small holes and watched Edgar. This was the first time I'd ever been alone with him. The salt-and-pepper hair on his head and chin needed a trim. I thought I would be nervous to be out here alone with him, but it surprised me to find he didn't scare me. Maybe it was because of everything we'd been through, but I realized Edgar was the least harsh of all the men in the other group. And to think, when he first married Mom, I thought *he* was the crazy one.

Finishing my drink, I handed the cup back to Edgar. After a while my fingers got cold, and I rubbed my hands together. Edgar stopped me, pointed to his ear, then out the window, and I gathered that the deer could hear the noise of my hands, so I sat on them instead.

We waited and watched until the darkness lightened. Edgar tapped my arm and pointed out the doorway. A deer had come into view and was busy peeling the bark off a tree trunk. Edgar handed me his bag and slowly poked his gun out one window and rested it on the old wood of the hut. He looked into the scope on top of his rifle and the world seemed to stop as I glanced from the deer, to Edgar, and back again.

BANG!

Despite the earmuffs, the noise of the gun startled me.

"Come on," Edgar said in his normal tone as he climbed out of the hut. In my shock, I'd momentarily forgotten about the deer, but I grabbed my gun and followed Edgar out of the hut. There was no deer in sight, but Edgar walked toward the place where the deer had been at a quick pace. I scrambled after him.

The first thing I saw was blood. There wasn't a lot, but the bright red spot on the white snow drew my attention. The animal wasn't there.

Edgar sighed. "We'll have to hunt it down and find it, so it doesn't have to suffer too long, and so the wolves don't get to it. We have to move fast, so keep up."

For the next ten minutes we followed the blood trail, which led us through a stream that got so deep Edgar had to carry me to the other side.

"Finally," he said, stopping short.

The snow was deeper here, so I'd been carefully placing my feet in the holes his steps had made, and I almost ran into him.

The large animal lay motionless on the ground, one of its front legs twisted awkwardly underneath it, the other stretched out straight.

Edgar lifted the deer's back legs and set them down again. "We'll need help getting this beauty back to the house. Let's go, so we can get back before other animals get our deer."

He took off toward the house, and I ran after him. Since we weren't worried anymore about how much noise we made, we took less time to make it back to the house.

I ran after him as fast as I could, but he beat me to the house by quite a distance as the water from the stream froze me and weighed me down.

When I got to the house, Chris and Edgar were ready to head back out on four-wheelers. Chris brought a long pole with him.

"What's that for?" I asked.

"We'll tie the deer to the pole so it will be easier to carry it. Why don't you get cleaned up and into dry clothes, and when we get back, I'll teach you how to skin it," said Chris.

Nodding, I trudged to the back porch, peeled off my boots and socks, then hiked up my pants so I wouldn't track mud into the house.

I was clean and dressed by the time they brought the dead animal inside the gate, set the pole down and untied the deer. They tied the rope around each back leg and hoisted it up so it hung from a tree, legs spread apart. Edgar paused and looked at me. "Are you going to get sick?"

"What are you going to do?"

"We have to gut the deer and drain the blood."

I shrugged. I had no idea how I would react.

He nodded, placed a bucket under the tail, then took a big knife from his belt and sliced the deer from the tail to just under the ribs. My stomach felt queasy, and I backed up a few feet.

Edgar wiped his knife on an old rag hanging from his belt, then reached his hands inside the dead carcass to pull the insides out.

I backed away even more.

"Intestines, stomach, lungs …" Chris pointed to each organ as he named them, and curiosity forced my feet closer.

"Time to skin it. Do you still want to learn how?" Chris asked.

I watched Edgar work for a little longer before answering. The process fascinated me, but I felt sorry for the deer, too.

"Yeah, I do," I said finally.

Chris motioned for me to come closer, and I did, standing near Edgar.

After washing his hands, Edgar showed me how to pull the fur tightly, then carefully run the knife where the skin joins with the meat.

"Want to try?" asked Edgar.

"Yeah!"

He handed me the knife and moved so I could take his place. Stretching the fur like I'd seen him do, I put the knife where I thought I should cut, and looked at Edgar before I did anything more. "Like this?"

"Yep, just pull the fur a little tighter, and go slow when you make the cut so you don't cut into the meat."

I adjusted and made my first cut. The skin came away smoothly, and I grinned. "I did it!"

Edgar nodded. "Keep going, I'll pull on the fur and you can slice away.

I skinned the left leg before my arm got too tired, and then I let Edgar take over again.

When all the skin was removed, they cut the meat into chunks. At that point, I ran back to the house to wash my hands and tell Jamie about my day. As I lathered my hands with soap, I heard Mom and Jamie arguing in the living room. I quickly rinsed my hands and turned the water off, hoping to hear them better.

"You're running from a custody case? Do you have any idea how much trouble Chris and I could get in if the police find out we've been hiding you here?"

"I don't want to lose my girls," said Mom.

"Sounds like you've already lost one. You're entangled with the government big time, and I'm not sure I'm comfortable with that."

Jamie sounded mad. Would she want us to leave? Why did Mom lie to her about Sapphira? Why did Mom always mess things up? This place was perfect; I didn't want to go.

Jamie walked into the kitchen a few seconds later and saw me. "How was the hunt?" she asked, trying to look interested, but I could tell she was struggling to hide her irritation with Mom.

"Great, I had a lot of fun. They showed me how to gut and skin the deer, and I did the whole left leg. I would have done more, but my arm got tired."

She gave my shoulder a friendly squeeze. "That's great, I'm glad you had fun. I'm headed out in a bit. I'll see you all in the morning."

Chapter 27

On the morning of Christmas Eve, I woke, as usual, before anyone in my family did and rushed upstairs. I loved having Jamie all to myself in the morning, sitting over our breakfast plates, chatting about whatever.

A heaping plate of food already sat at my usual seat. Jamie stood at the counter pouring herself a cup of coffee, then she joined me at the table. "Good morning, do you know what today is?"

"It's Christmas Eve," I said, picking up the steaming cup of hot chocolate she'd made for me.

"Have you been a good girl this year?" she asked.

"As good as I could be, but I guess it depends on who you ask," I said, thinking about Stewart.

Jamie grinned. "Well, if you ask me, you've been a perfect angel."

I smiled and for a few minutes we ate in silence, both lost in our own thoughts.

"Sophia, when you first got here, you seemed afraid to say or do anything for fear of getting in trouble, but you've opened up a lot. Are you comfortable here? Do you feel safe?" asked Jamie.

I looked at her curiously, remembering the argument she'd had with Mom a couple of days ago and wondering, again, if they were going to make us leave. "I am comfortable, and I feel happier. I love that Chris and Edgar are teaching me how to defend myself. That helps make me feel safe. And you and Chris are really nice, and I like you a lot," I said, unable to make eye contact with her as I spoke.

Jamie didn't respond, so I looked up and found her smiling at me with tears in her eyes. "I'm glad I met you, Sophia, and that we've been able to help you feel safer and happier, and I know God will take care of you on your life's journey, no matter where you are. I think you and your sister have both been good girls, and I think Santa is going to bring you presents."

"Thanks, Jamie," I said, and we finished our meal in silence.

Mom was her normal self today and spent the day watching us do tricks on the trampoline and playing games with us. I hadn't heard her laugh so much in a long time. Eva and I had a hard time falling asleep that night in anticipation of Christmas morning. Jamie seemed so sure that I'd let go of my doubts and allowed myself to get excited.

Christmas Day came. Everyone woke up early, and when we went upstairs we found a beautifully decorated Christmas tree with presents underneath it. Jamie and Chris sat on the couch near the tree, smiling at us as we joined them in the living room.

"Looks like I guessed right. You've both been good this year," said Jamie.

"See, Sophia, I told you Santa had enough magic to find us!" said Eva.

Mom hugged us both, and I noticed she had tears in her eyes. "Let's find out what Santa brought my good girls."

"Yeah, let's see what we have under here," said Chris, who slid off the couch and sat cross-legged on the floor beside the tree. He grabbed a present and looked at the tag, "To Eva from Santa. Here you go, little one." And he handed it to her.

She squealed in delight and tore the wrapping off it. "It's a new baby doll!" she yelled with delight and started tearing off the cardboard around it. Her little fingers found the task difficult, and she went to Mom and Edgar to help her get it out of the box.

Everyone laughed at her excitement.

Chris picked up a long, rectangular present with a smaller present attached to it and read, "To Sophia from Santa." He handed me the box and I tested its weight in my hands. It was pretty heavy.

I took off the smaller box and set it aside before ripping the paper off the larger one. It was a pump-action BB gun with a cleaning kit, and the smaller gift was a bottle of coppery BBs. I was speechless.

Jamie knelt down beside me and gave me a hug, "Now you have your own gun to defend yourself," she whispered to me and kissed my cheek.

"Thank you," I said with a hoarse voice, certain she'd told Santa about where we were, so we wouldn't miss Christmas.

"Wow, Sophia, that is a pretty cool gift," said Mom. Edgar, sitting beside her, nodded his head in agreement.

"Yeah, it is. Sophia, did you see my new baby? I think I'm going to call her Sapphira because I miss my big sister," said Eva.

Tears filled my eyes. "Hi, baby Sapphira, welcome to the family," I said, giving the doll a kiss. Clutching my gun to my chest, I sat watching Eva play with her doll while the adults talked and exchanged their own gifts.

"Why don't you girls go get dressed, then Jamie and I will show Sophia how to load, clean and shoot that gun," said Chris.

"I would love that," I said, scrambling to my feet and running downstairs.

Chris took me to the back porch and showed me how to take the whole gun apart and put it back together. He let me practice a few times, and it was pretty easy once I got the hang of it. Then he showed me where to load the BBs.

Jamie took me outside, where she'd set up some targets. "Pay attention to how I do this, Sophia." She pulled back the loading action and shot it. "That's all there is to it. Now, you try."

It was a little hard to pull back because the barrel was longer than my arm, but eventually it came back with a click. Placing the butt of the gun on my shoulder like they taught me, I pulled the trigger.

The gun kicked back just like a real shotgun, but not as hard. I hadn't expected it, but I loved it.

"Well done! Did you feel the recoil?" asked Jamie.

I nodded.

"We wanted you to get a feel for what a real shotgun would feel like," Jamie said.

I grinned. They'd gotten to know me so well since I'd been here. "Mom!" I yelled inside the house. "You have to come try this!"

She joined me and tried the gun for herself, missing the target every time. "That is very cool, baby, it feels like a real gun. You enjoy your new toy. I'm going to go back inside with Eva."

"I think we should head inside, too," said Jamie. "Chris can show you how to clean the gun."

Chris was waiting on the back porch with the cleaning supplies. I took the gun apart like he'd showed me, and we spent an hour going over each part and how to clean and oil them. "If you use too much oil it's bad, so only use little drops at a time. Do you have any questions?"

"Yes. Where is the safety on this?" I asked.

Chris smiled. "Good question. It's this button on the trigger. Push it to the left for armed, then push it to the right for disarmed."

"Thanks. Can I take it out and keep practicing with it?"

"Sure. I'll come out and check on you periodically. Have fun."

"Can I try to shoot it?" asked Eva.

I glanced at Chris, who shrugged. "Okay."

We spent several hours taking turns with the BB gun, and I showed Eva everything Chris and Edgar had taught me, except how to shoot to kill.

Jamie made a big, early dinner of ham, potatoes, salad, stuffing, and two pies for dessert. We told stories about past Christmases and laughed. After, Mom, Eva and I sat on the couch while the others cleaned up. Eva busied herself with her doll, changing it into the extra outfit that came with it. I grabbed a candy cane off the tree to eat.

"Why can't we go home?" asked Eva.

"We just can't," said Mom.

"Did Sapphira go back home?" asked Eva.

Mom's lip trembled. "No, baby."

"Then where—"

"Eva, did you open your candy cane yet?" I asked.

Mom got up and headed toward the basement.

"No, I'm saving mine," said Eva.

Jamie walked in with a board game. "Would you girls like to play a game?"

We both said yes to this suggestion and followed Jamie back to the kitchen. We helped her set up the game at the table.

"Eight o'clock, girls, time for bed," said Jamie as we wrapped up our third game of Sorry. We helped clean up the game and headed downstairs. Mom appeared to be sleeping, but she was facing the wall, so it was hard to tell. After tucking in my little sister, I climbed to the top bunk, snuggled under my blankets, and allowed myself to think about Sapphira.

Was she with the others again? Why hadn't she gone home? Where else could she be? Was she still pregnant? And why couldn't we go home? Jamie had said something about a "custody case" when I overheard them talking the other day, but I didn't know what that meant. When we left, I thought we were leaving because Edgar was in trouble with the law, but Jamie seemed to think Mom was the one in trouble.

Chapter 28

1 Month Before The FBI Standoff

A month wonderful month of playing in the snow, shooting my gun, and helping Jamie passed quickly. I asked Jamie for permission to go into the tree house, but she said no. A fresh blanket of snow had fallen overnight, and she worried the ladder would be icy.

Eva and I made snowmen and had a snowball fight. There wasn't enough snow to make forts, so we hid behind the snowmen we'd built. After an hour, we were too cold to keep playing outdoors. All of our clothes had holes in them by now, and we didn't have winter coats, only jackets.

"Goodness, girls, look at your little red cheeks and noses. How about some hot chocolate to warm you up?" asked Jamie.

We agreed happily and sipped at the warm beverage as we huddled under a blanket on the couch.

"Since it's so cold outside today, how would you girls like to help me with some projects around the house?"

Both of us agreed, and Jamie put us to work. She handed Eva an old sock and a can of dust spray.

"Put this on your hand, spray a little of the dust spray onto the sock, then wipe the wood furniture in the living room, okay?"

Eva laughed. "I've never dusted with a sock before."

Jamie smiled and pointed out the furniture that needed dusting.

"Now, Sophia, I have some chairs that need repairing. Can you help me with that?"

"Sure."

I followed her to the garage, where she pointed out two chairs, one with a broken armrest and another with two broken legs.

"Let's carry these to the kitchen, where it's warmer and there's more light."

Once they were in the kitchen, she started with the chair that had the broken arm.

"First, we need to sand these splinters off, then we can glue it back together."

"How did this break?" I asked.

"Not sure. I found this set of chairs in a garbage pile. The ones around the table were perfectly fine, but these two were broken, and I haven't had a chance to fix them until now."

Jamie handed me a small sheet of sanding paper and showed me how to use it.

I smoothed the broken edges. Jamie held it up to the chair to see how it would fit before applying wood glue to it.

"There will be a big crack after you glue it," I said.

"We'll put a lot of glue in there so it seeps out the sides. When it's dry, we'll cut off the big chunks and sand it down. You won't even be able to tell."

"I didn't know you could sand glue."

She smiled at me. "Here, hold these together while I figure out how to clamp these."

I held the pieces together while she arranged two clamps and some rope to keep the chair pieces in place. With that arranged, we moved on to the second chair. This one was easy. We set the chair upside-down on the table so the back part hung off the side. We only had to glue the legs back into their holes and didn't need to clamp them.

Eva finished her job before we did and stood in the middle of the kitchen, watching. The sock, hanging limply from her hand, was now black with dirt.

"All right, girls, thanks for your help. Ready for the next project?"

Before we could respond, Edgar burst through the front door. "Grace, we have to leave—now," yelled Edgar.

"What's going on?" asked Chris.

"Police, one down the street, another around the block. A third one followed me into the neighborhood and stopped to chat with the one around the corner. I think they've found us," Edgar said.

"Dammit, they're going to raid the place," said Jamie. "All of you, get in the tree house right now. I'll hide your things."

"How do you know they'll raid it?" asked Mom.

"I told you, Grace, we keep to ourselves, we're off the grid. The government can't monitor us here. If they suspect you're here, they'll use that as an excuse to come in here and find out what we're doing. Now, if you want to keep your two girls, you'll get up in the tree house now," she snapped.

The image of Sapphira being taken away came to my mind. I grabbed Eva's hand and pulled her toward the back door. If Mom wanted to stay behind and discuss the matter, fine, but I would listen to Jamie.

"Shouldn't we leave?" asked Edgar. "We can—"

"Only if you want to be found," said Chris.

It was freezing outside, but I forced Eva to run beside me and made her climb up the boards on the tree ahead of me. I'd started climbing when Mom and Edgar ran up, panting, behind me. There was snow on the rungs and it made them slippery, so the climb was slow going.

Reaching the top, I looked over the side and saw flashes of red and blue lights below, but I couldn't see or hear anything else.

"Edgar, what do you think will happen?" asked Mom.

"I don't know, but Chris and Jamie will know what to do, they'll take care of it."

"What about our things? Our clothes, the girls' toys, they were all over the basement floor," said Mom.

"Don't worry, Grace. I told you, Chris and Jamie will take care of it," Edgar said.

I sat toward the front of the tree house to watch the flashing lights.

"Mom, I'm getting cold," said Eva.

"I know, baby. Be patient."

Several minutes passed in silence.

"Girls, why don't we pretend something to pass the time," said Mom.

"Like what?" Eva asked.

"Let's see … we could pretend we're a pack of animals surviving in the wild."

"Can we be wolves?" I asked.

"Yeah, wolves!" Eva chimed in.

"Okay, we can be wolves, but we have to be quiet wolves," Mom said. "No howling."

"We need a wolf name," I said.

"Like what?"

"How about the wolverines?"

"That is perfect," said Mom.

"I want to be the daughter wolf, and Mom can be the mom wolf, and Sophia, you can be the sister wolf," Eva said.

"As long as I can be the wolf who goes hunting for our food, then I'm cool with that."

Mom pretended to bathe Eva with her tongue to get her ready for wolf school and I climbed up to the second deck of the tree house. "This can be the hunting grounds."

After a few minutes, I climbed down, pretending to carry a dead rabbit in my mouth. I set it next to Mom and Eva, and we pretended to rip it to pieces.

We played as quietly as possible until we could no longer ignore how cold we were. Then we huddled together, watched the lights, and tried to keep each other warm. Time passed slowly, and I was sure it was well past midnight before the lights disappeared.

"It looks like they're leaving now," I whispered. "How will we know when we can go down?"

"I'm sure one of them will come and tell us," said Edgar.

An eternity later, the trapdoor of the tree house opened, and Chris popped his head through. "It's safe to come down now."

I shook Eva, who'd fallen asleep. My legs were stiff from sitting and the cold, and it was hard to climb down while shivering, but we all made it safely to the ground.

Back in the house, we found our bags sitting next to the garage door.

"Jamie is scouting the neighborhood. In the morning, we'll get you somewhere safe. I think we convinced them it's just us here, but they might come back," Chris said.

Edgar nodded. "Thank you for sheltering us for this long."

The two men shook hands. "I'm glad we got rid of your truck and got you a new vehicle when you got here," Chris said.

I sat on a chair in the kitchen. We were leaving again.

Edgar grabbed the bags and took them outside to the car. A few minutes later, Jamie returned. "No one is watching the place. I'll make some calls tonight, and we'll have you safe in Montana by tomorrow."

"Thank you for everything, Jamie," Edgar said.

She nodded.

I hugged her waist tight and hoped she would say we could stay with her, but she only hugged me back. Why did we have to leave every place I loved?

The next morning, the doorbell rang several times before breakfast. I climbed out of bed and headed upstairs to see who the visitors were, hoping they weren't cops or social workers. People filled the living room and kitchen, many of them men with long beards, biker vests, and bandanas tied round their heads. Jamie and some other women were in the kitchen, cooking.

"Good morning, sunshine," said Jamie. "Come sit and eat. You have a long day ahead of you."

Mom, Edgar, and Eva came upstairs shortly after I did.

"Who are all these people?" Edgar asked.

"Friends," said Chris. "They'll help you get to Montana."

"Everyone, listen up! Our guests have joined us, and I want to make sure we're all on the same page," yelled an older man with a gray handlebar mustache.

The room quieted, more people crowded into the kitchen, and the gray-mustached man continued.

"These folks need to get to the compound, and we're going to help them. We have thirty cars, so we'll have ten in front and ten in back, watching for police. The other ten will surround the car and make sure they're okay along the way. As soon as you eat this delicious meal Jamie and the girls have made, head out to your vehicles and wait for my signal. We'll use channel five on the radios to communicate. Understood?"

Several people grunted or nodded their heads.

"Great, let's eat!" said Chris.

The clatter of dishes and clamor of voices was overwhelming. It reminded me of the school cafeteria at lunchtime, and that felt like a lifetime ago.

"Are you coming with us?" I asked Jamie as I placed my plate in the sink.

"No, if Chris and I go, the police could come back and take our home. We have to stay and protect it. You'll be okay, Sophia. We will talk again someday, I'm sure. Be good and stay out of trouble."

I hugged her. "I'll miss you."

"Aw, I'll miss you too, little Sophia." Jamie kissed the top of my head. "Now, you better get outside. They'll be leaving soon."

Fifteen minutes later, we were on the road, surrounded by Jamie and Chris's friends. We drove all day, stopped in a campground for the night, then drove another two hours before reaching Montana, but everyone stayed with us on the long drive.

We turned onto a dirt road, crossed over a cattle guard, and passed a sign that said, "Freedom Township." I wrote it down in my notebook, under the list I'd been making of places we'd been. I didn't know all the cities or states, but I described them the best I could. This would be the tenth place in almost five months. Home felt more like a dream than somewhere I'd lived most of my life.

"Mom, where are we?" asked Eva.

I bent forward a little, so I could hear over the noise of the truck engine and the popping, crackling sounds of the tires on dirt and rock.

"We're on a safe ranch. No one can get us here."

Eva looked at me, one eyebrow raised.

I shrugged. "We'll find out soon." There weren't many trees here. Instead, there were mountains around us and it felt a little more like home, which made my heart ache a little.

We pulled up to a big white house that had a pole near the entrance. An American flag attached to it flapped in the wind. There were three windows on the front of the building, flanked by blue shutters.

Mountains surrounded the ranch. Fences marked off sections of the land like they might have cattle, or horses, but I didn't see any animals.

"I have to pee. Can I go inside there?" I asked, climbing out of the truck.

"Yes, be quick, and don't wander off," Edgar said.

I was surprised to walk into a lobby instead of a living room. Gun safes lined the wall on the right, and chairs lined the wall on the left. In the middle of the room stood a reception desk with a vase of fake flowers. Two men, both wearing jeans and cowboy boots, sat near the desk, waiting for who knows what. On the wall behind the desk hung a giant American flag. *They sure like our flag here.*

"Welcome. Are your parents here?" asked one of the men. He was bald and had a long, white beard and brown eyes.

"Yes, outside. I'm looking for the bathroom. Can you tell me where it is?"

Smiling, he pointed to a doorway. "Through there, to the left, at the end of the hallway."

"Thank you."

Glass cases lined the hallway and pictures covered the walls. I meandered along, taking in everything: old military pictures, the

Declaration of Independence, old guns, letters, and war medals. *This place must be a museum.*

I found the bathroom, did my business, and made my way back to the lobby, knowing Mom wouldn't be happy I was taking so long.

"Sophia?" The bald man stood when I came back in.

How did he know my name?

"Your mom asked me to show you where to go when you finished. I'm Kevin, by the way."

"Oh, okay. Why is all that stuff in the hallway?"

"Well, the pictures and items all document our history and our rights as a nation. The government is trying to take our rights away from us, which is why we've created this safe place. We'll teach you and your family how to defend yourself."

He led me across the lobby to a set of double doors and opened one. "Your mom is right over there."

Rows of chairs filled the room. Opposite from where I stood was a podium, centered on a small stage. A man stood at the podium, talking. Mom sat on the front row and waved at me when I came in.

I pointed to a chair on the back row, then to myself, before taking a seat. I listened intently to the man who spoke, trying to figure out what kind of people we were to stay with. He talked about our rights to freedom of speech and listed several ways the government had taken that right away from us.

I lay down across several chairs. They weren't talking about all the crazy things the other group had talked about, but it was still weird government stuff. In a few minutes I was asleep.

"Sophia, wake up." Mom's voice sounded far away, but when I opened my eyes, she was standing over me, and next to her was the man from the lobby. "Let's go, Kevin is taking us to our cabin."

A cabin?! I sat up fully awake. This would be fun.

We followed the dirt road to a crossroad. Kevin stopped and pointed to the left. "Over that way are some trailer homes, a barn, and a field where we grow and keep some of our supplies. There's also a big, abandoned ship over there that the kids might like to explore sometime. Just keep an eye out for rat traps.

"Behind the trailer homes is a corral with horses. Other than that, it is just mainly fields of weeds and grass. Eventually we'll use that land for growing crops; we just haven't gotten around to preparing the soil yet. There isn't much to the right, except another exit off the ranch. Straight ahead are the cabins."

He started forward again. The road curved left and down a hill, where a small lake came into view on our right. Three cabins stood in a row several yards from the lake. A fourth cabin looked to be about a mile walk from the others. We stopped at the third cabin in the row.

"If you keep going down this road," said Kevin, climbing out of the car, "you'd go back up the hill a ways down there and meet up with this road we just came down. It's a big circle."

The cabins appeared identical from the outside. They were made of tree trunks that had been cut in half and placed strategically, one atop the other. Between each log was something that looked like tar from off the highways. The cabins were stained a dark brown, almost black color, and every other log stuck out on each side of the house. I could climb to the roof if I wanted to.

"This last cabin will be yours," said Kevin. "Pull on that leather cord there by the door to open it. When you're inside, pull the cord through the hole, and no one will get in unless they kick down the door. Even that will be difficult. We build these little places solid. If you're really in a bind, the hole where the leather comes through is big enough to fit the barrel of a shotgun."

The sun was fading quickly as I walked up to the door and pulled the leather rope, which felt like a horse lead. This place was fascinating. Inside, on the left, was a small kitchen. On the right, a small hide-a-bed couch. Past the kitchen was a door that led to a bedroom, and down a little hall to the right was the bathroom. It had one window that opened inward.

"You girls get the couch, and your mom and I get the bedroom," Edgar said.

Mom pulled the bed out and made it while Eva and I changed into jammies, then she tucked us in and kissed our foreheads. "Goodnight, my babies."

Since I had slept most of the drive, as usual, I had a hard time sleeping that first night. Everyone called this place a "safe ranch." Jamie and Chris were connected to these people somehow, and I felt safe and loved at their house. Plus, no one from the other group where Sapphira was taken away was here. I thought I should accept that I was safe here; it was a huge place. Sure, the cabin was small, but I could explore the area for days and still find new places, which meant lots of places to hide. Lots of *safe* places to find. But until I knew these people better, I couldn't relax. I had to keep my guard up and keep Eva close.

Chapter 29

Just as I was finally drifting off to sleep, Mom made a muffled, screeching noise from the bedroom and I sat upright. What was Edgar doing to her? The image of Stewart holding a big sword to Sapphira's throat flashed through my mind. Their door was open a crack, so I climbed out of bed and tiptoed over. If he was hurting her, what would I do? I could knock on one of the other cabin doors, but did anyone live in them? I hadn't noticed earlier. Where had Edgar put my BB gun when we got here?

Cautiously, I peered through the opening. My eyes were still adjusting to the dark, but it looked like someone's butt was sticking up in the air.

"Mom? Are you okay?" I asked, pushing the door open a little more.

They both laughed. "I'm okay, baby, shut the door and go back to bed."

As she spoke, I realized it was Edgar's butt I was seeing, and they were both naked. I turned away quickly.

"Oh gross! You guys are disgusting!" I slammed the door closed and ran back to bed as quickly as I could in the dark. The image of Edgar's pasty white butt was burned into my mind, and I wanted to barf.

"What's going on?" asked Eva. She sniffed and wiped tears from her eyes.

I snuggled under the blankets again and pulled her to me. "Nothing. Mom was just being dumb. Sorry I scared you."

She wrapped her arms around me, and soon we were both asleep.

Pots and pans banging on the stove woke me the next morning.

"Oh good, you're awake. Breakfast is almost ready," said Mom.

Eva climbed out of bed and ran to the bathroom. I had to pee, too, so I got up and folded the blankets to distract myself. Mom put the couch bed away, and I put the blankets on top. Eva still hadn't finished.

"Are you almost done in there? I need to pee."

"Go away, I'm busy," said Eva.

Since when did she get so bossy? I stood near the door and waited. Edgar came out of the bedroom, and the image of his butt appeared in my mind. I shuddered. How could Mom stand to see him naked?

"I'm off to the main house. I'll find something to eat later," he said as he walked outside.

The toilet flushed, and a moment later Eva came out. "I'm done. Enjoy the smell," she said cheekily and hurried to the kitchen.

I wrinkled my nose as I walked in, but the only thing I smelled was a faint metallic odor, but I played along to make Eva laugh.

"Oh gosh, what did you eat, Eva? It smells like something died in here! Mom, do we have any spray?"

They both burst out laughing. "Sorry, baby, you'll have to open the window."

When I rejoined the others, Eva grinned at me. "Did you enjoy my good morning present to you?"

I smiled, shook my head, and grabbed a bowl Mom set on the counter. Oatmeal. Gross. "Do we have any sugar?"

"Not right now, just eat it fast."

I took big bites so it would disappear quicker, but I had to force myself to swallow the flavorless mush.

"You girls can go out and play, but I want you to stay in sight of the cabins for now," Mom said.

There wasn't much to explore. The lake might be fun to fish in at some point, but we had no poles at the moment and were not allowed around it unless Mom was with us. Behind the cabins was a mountain of dirt. At the top of the dirt hill was the road that passed by the cabins and circled around to the trailer homes. Eva and I grabbed my trucks from the cabin and played in the dirt with them all day, looking for treasures.

"Soph, check this out. It's huge!" said Eva.

I ran over to see what she had found. A big rock that looked like it had specks of diamonds in it poked out of the earth. We spent the next half an hour trying to free the stone from the dirt. When we got it out, it looked like a big dinosaur foot, with gemstones all over it.

"Let's go show Mom!" shouted Eva excitedly.

We ran to the front of the cabin and through the door and found Mom sitting on the couch, staring into space.

"Look, Mom, we found a shiny dinosaur foot. I bet it's worth millions of dollars. Can we keep it?" I asked.

Mom nodded her head slowly, her thoughts seemingly far away. "That's great." Her words slurred a little.

Ever since she got sick at the farmhouse, she hadn't been herself. I watched Mom a few more minutes before joining Eva. Watching her, I realized we needed to get out of here, not just for my sake and Eva's, but for Mom's, too.

After a week, Eva and I were allowed to explore the ranch a little more, but we had our boundaries. Mom came with us most of the time and I was glad. The area around the cabins was boring, and it was just us three having fun, without any big rules or church crap. One day I saw a guy fishing in the lake and ran back to our cabin to ask Mom if I could fish, too.

"Sure, let's see if we can find you a pole."

Mom walked with me and Eva to the cabin standing by itself at the end of the lake and knocked on the door. It was the only cabin, besides ours, that anyone lived in.

"Hey, Daniel," Mom said when a young man opened the door. "Do you have an extra fishing pole my daughter can use?"

Daniel was much younger than the other men who lived on the ranch. He had beautiful blue eyes and dark hair, and his arms were all muscle. I wouldn't admit it to anyone, but I thought he was pretty cute.

"Sure, let me get it ready for you." He disappeared inside his cabin and came back out a few minutes later with a pole. "Have fun."

"Thank you," I said.

I made my way to a muddy bank to look for worms.

"Over here, Sophia," Mom said.

"I need worms."

"No, you don't. There is a trap over here with live minnows in it. You can use them as bait." She showed me the trap, submerged in water and brimming with tiny fish.

"How do they get in there? Can't they just swim back out?" I asked.

"I'm not sure. Who cares? Do you want to fish or not?"

"Yes."

"Great, then grab a minnow, put it on your hook, and be quiet so the fish aren't scared away."

I did as she told me, and once I'd cast my line, she retreated to sit under a tree where Eva was sitting with her dolls to watch. The man I saw earlier was fishing nearby, but it didn't look like he was having much luck catching anything.

I sat watching the water for any signs of fish for at least ten minutes before I saw a big one jump out of the water near the man. I quickly reeled in my line and moved closer to him before casting again.

A few minutes later, I had a bite. "Mom, Mom, I got a fish!" I tried to reel it in, but the fish was so big I had to sit on the ground and dig my heels into the dirt to keep from sliding toward the water.

The man who'd been fishing nearby threw down his pole, grabbed a net and ran to help me. By the time he got there I had reeled the fish in enough that it was splashing in the shallow water by the shore. There was a one-foot ledge from the bank to the water, and the man lay down on the ground so he could catch the fish in the net.

The fish was so big it filled the net and part of its head and tail were sticking out of it.

The man and I caught our breath and watched the fish flop around in the net.

"Hey, little girl, that was quite a catch. I've been trying to hook this guy all morning. Do you mind if I have it?" he asked.

I thought for a moment. We'd been eating oatmeal every meal since we got here. This fish would be the first tasty thing I'd eaten in a week. "Sorry, you can't have it. I don't want to eat any more oatmeal."

The man looked at Mom, who'd walked over during all the excitement.

"Sorry, she caught it fair and square. It's her fish," said Mom.

The man stood up, threw his hat on the ground, stomped on it and let out a stream of curse words before walking back to his pole, picking it up and storming away.

"Wow, Mom, that guy needs a time out," said Eva.

"Yep. Let's go," said Mom. "Edgar can show you how to gut the fish. He's over by Daniel's place now, and we can return the fishing pole too."

We met Edgar by the minnow net and showed him the fish.

"Great catch. That is the biggest rainbow trout I've ever seen. Let's gut and clean this beauty," Edgar said.

"And I'll return Daniel's pole while you do that," Mom said.

I followed him to the edge of the lake, where he took a knife from a pouch attached to his belt. "Okay, first you put the pointy part of the knife in the lower part of the belly, by the fin. Make sure the knife slants up a little so you don't cut your fingers. Slice until the knife is to the gills." He made the cut.

"Next, pull the head towards the fin. You should be able to get all the insides out at once if you do it right. If not, just run your thumb along the spine from fin to head and be sure to throw the guts aside for another animal to eat."

"That's gross," said Mom, who had just joined us again. She still had the fishing pole.

Edgar grinned and winked at her.

"You're such a man," said Mom, walking away. "Oh, Sophia, Daniel said you could keep this pole, so I'll take it back to the cabin," she yelled over her shoulder.

"Now that the gutting is done, we'll take it up to the house to clean and descale it," Edgar said.

He handed me the fish, and we walked back to the cabin. It felt much lighter now that it didn't have all of its guts. Edgar showed me how to rinse the fish and wrap it in tinfoil. "We'll put lemon, butter, salt and pepper in with it and let it sit in the fridge to marinate until dinner time. Great work."

"Thank you."

"Here, I think you're ready for this." Edgar reached into his pocket, pulled out a red object and handed it to me.

I took it and ran my fingers over the word "Swiss" painted along one edge.

"It's a pocket knife."

I knew what it was. I'd wanted one since the one I'd found in the yellow trailer home had gone missing. "Thank you," I said, carefully pulling out each of the tiny tools to inspect them.

"Be careful with that. The knife is especially sharp. That's not a kid's knife. Grace, I'm going out with the others to hunt. I'll be back for dinner," Edgar said.

I strapped the knife holder onto my belt and went outside to experiment with my new tools.

That evening, we ate fish and rice. The white meat with a slight tang of lemon melted in my mouth. All it took was a short time fishing to get this amazing meal. I would never eat oatmeal again. This experience taught me there is always another way to get food. *If I grow up poor, I will simply find a stream and go fishing. If I grow up and have a million dollars, I will ban all gross foods from my house.*

"Girls, take a shower tonight before you go to bed," Mom said. "We're going to the white house tomorrow morning and I want you clean. We'll meet everyone living here and find new things to learn, then we'll be free to explore any area of the ranch you want."

Eva and I high-fived.

Chapter 30

"Let's go!" Edgar shouted from outside.

I finished tying Eva's shoes, and we rushed outside and climbed into the car.

"This will be a little like school," he said. "They'll have lots of different things for you to learn how to do."

"Something other than times tables?"

Mom slapped my knee. "Those people took good care of us, and you should be thankful they had any schooling for you at all."

I rolled my eyes. Oh yes, they took such great care of us that Sapphira was taken away. Had Mom forgotten that part? Could she really be so clueless about everything they did to us?

"This is a school for everyone. Kids and adults. Everyone has a job here, and we'll be learning all the different jobs so we can help keep things safe in their family dynamic of militia members," Edgar explained.

"So we have to get a job?" I asked.

Eva groaned, "I'm not cleaning out any more horse stalls."

"No, babies, you don't have to get a job. Not yet, anyway, but you might find something interesting to learn. Like a hobby," Mom said.

"What's a hobby?" asked Eva.

"It's an activity people like to do. Like collecting dinosaur bones, or stamps."

"Collecting stamps? That sounds boring," said Eva.

"How does that help anyone?" I asked.

"It doesn't," Mom sighed. "I was just using that as an example of what a hobby is."

We pulled up to the white house and got out. Eva and I ran inside. Tables covered with many fascinating things were lined up near the walls, with people standing behind them ready to show anyone who came to them how to do the job they were describing. Eva ran off to watch a woman spinning yarn, and I went to a table with a bunch of containers.

"Hi there, I'm Brooke," the woman there said. "Would you like to learn how to make soap?"

"That sounds cool. Yes, please."

"Well, we start with fresh goat's milk. This batch came from my female goat, Pickles. We want the milk to be smooth, so we'll strain it. Would you hold the strainer for me?"

"Sure," I said, taking the handle of the strange pot-like thing she handed me. The bowl part was made of wire mesh. The holes were so tiny I didn't think anything would go through, but when Brooke poured the goat's milk, the liquid came out the other end and it felt like there wasn't any weight on the strainer.

"Great, thanks. Now, we have many choices when it comes to creating soap. We can add all kinds of oils to it that help our skin." Brook held up several bottles and containers and showed them to me. "For example, we will use olive oil, some coconut oil, and tallow. This is lye; we have to be very careful using it, because it can burn our skin." She stirred the mixture, then brought out some molds.

"Okay, this is the fun part." She took a ladle and added the white mixture into each mold, but didn't fill them all the way. "Now, all you have to do is add the flowers, herbs, oats or perfumes you want. I'll let you decide what to choose, but you have to wear these rubber gloves."

After examining the bowls, I put the gloves on, then stuffed lavender and mint leaves into the liquid until it reached the top of the mold.

"Great choice," Brooke said. "It will take twenty-four hours to process the soap, then it has to be exposed to the air every day for three weeks. So if you're still here, you can come get your masterpiece."

My shoulders sagged. As much as we moved around, there wasn't much chance I would ever get to see the soap I made.

I walked around to the other booths and met everyone. They had a woodworking table, which was my favorite, yarn making, weaving, and even a blacksmith who showed everyone how to make a horseshoe. At the end of the event, they called everyone into the meeting room and had my family stand at the front to welcome us to Freedom Township.

It was cool, but it also freaked me out. Kevin told everyone where we lived and asked all the people there to help Mom and Edgar keep us safe. As long as they weren't like Richard, Mike, or any of the other people who were supposed to keep us safe, it would be fine.

"Girls, let's go check out a house down the road. They have horses you can ride," Mom said the week after we met everyone.

"Do we have to clean up after them?" asked Eva.

"No, baby."

"Okay, then I'm in," said Eva.

Finally! Some horses we could interact with. I ran ahead of Mom, but since I didn't know where exactly I was going, I stopped every so often to let them catch up.

On the left side of the road was a ravine filled with trees. That must be where Edgar went hunting. To the right was the lake, and where the lake ended there was a big open space and then big cliffs. In the big open space was the ship Kevin told us about the day we arrived, though I'd forgotten about it since. It was tilted to one side a little, and the bottom was buried in dirt. Next to it was a big red barn.

We reached the end of the ravine and the road. To the left of us was a white trailer home, sitting by itself, and straight in front of us were two more of the same color. Behind these two was the horse corral.

"Did the lake used to be bigger?" I asked.

"I don't know, baby, why?"

"Because that ship looks like it's been there for a long time. I wondered if the lake dried up and that's why it's still there."

"Sounds like a good question for Hank."

"Who?"

"The man who owns the horses and this whole ranch." She pointed to the white trailer home standing by itself.

Veering toward the little, white, rectangular house, I stared at the ship as I walked, wondering if I would ever get the chance to explore it.

"Here we are," Mom said.

A young girl with long black hair opened the door. She smiled and waved at us. The woman I'd met at the soap-making station, Brooke, followed the girl out.

"You two are going to spend the day with Melissa while I work," Mom said.

"Melissa, this is Sophia and Eva. You girls have fun and stay out of trouble while Grace and I are working," Brooke said.

"Wait—I made soap yesterday. Will you get it from Brooke when it's ready?"

"I'll ask her about it," Mom said. "Love you both. I'll see you this evening. Sophia, look after your sister." Mom climbed into a green car with Brooke.

Great. Mom brought us up here so we would have a babysitter.

"Hi, it's nice to meet you," said Melissa.

I forced a smile. "It's nice to meet you, too. I'm Sophia, and this is Eva."

"Have you guys been to this part of the compound before?" asked Melissa.

"No, we haven't seen very much at all," I said.

"Well, why don't I take you on a tour. We can't go all over the compound, but I can show you this part of it."

We agreed to this and spend over an hour following Melissa while she showed us around.

"Do you want to go meet the horses?" asked Melissa when we finally returned to her house.

"We don't have to clean up their poop, do we?" asked Eva, who apparently didn't trust Mom's answer earlier. I couldn't blame her.

Melissa laughed. "No, come on."

We followed her over to a gate that served as the entrance to the corral. A man I recognized from the previous evening was trying to catch a horse with a rope and a whip, but it didn't look like he was having much success. There was a colt, too, which was keeping as far away from the cracking whip as it could get.

"That's my grandpa, Hank," said Melissa.

Shaking my head at Hank's attempts, I walked closer to the fence. "Watch this," I said to Melissa and Eva, then climbed over the gate.

"Be careful," said Melissa. "That one has a temper."

"I will."

"Don't run, or the colt over there will think you're playing," said Hank, as I walked up next to him. He'd stopped chasing the horse when he saw me climb over the gate.

"What are you doing?" I asked.

"Well, I'm trying to catch this horse so I can saddle her for a ride. She needs exercise," he said, breathing heavily.

"What's her name?"

"Beauty."

"That's a pretty name," I said.

The horse was completely black, except for rings of white on her feet. Hank bent over and put his hands on his knees, still trying to catch his breath. He was a grandpa, all right. He had white hair sticking out from his brown cowboy hat and wore light jeans with suspenders that kept his pants up around his big belly. He was definitely too old to be catching such a spirited horse.

"Can I try?" I asked.

"Sure kid," he chuckled. "You'll need this whip. She doesn't like being caught."

I stared at the whip in his hand. I wouldn't know how to use it correctly, and besides it was a mean way to get a horse to do something. I had an overwhelming sense of love for Beauty. What did this mean?

"No thanks. Can I have the lead for her halter?" I asked.

Hank handed me the requested item, shaking his head. I turned to face the horse. Clicking my tongue and staring at her right in those big, beautiful, brown eyes, I strolled toward her. "Hi, beautiful girl, it's okay," I said quietly.

Beauty ran from me, and I just kept walking towards her slowly, with the lead behind my back. "It's okay, I won't hurt you." She stopped once at the gate I'd climbed over and turned to look at me. Something told me I should stop and wait, so I did. She took two steps toward me. I held out my hand and waited. When she was within arm's reach, I attached the lead to her halter. "Good girl," I said, stroking her neck as she sniffed my hair.

I led her back to Hank, who stared wide-eyed at me. "How the heck did you do that?"

"You just have to be nice to her, and she'll be nice to you." I scratched behind her ears and covered her neck and nose in kisses.

Mom finished early and was at the gate with Eva and Melissa when I walked the horse back with Hank to the corral entrance.

"Can we go see the baby horse?" asked Eva.

"Sure, Melissa will keep an eye on you while I take Beauty for her exercise," Hank said. "He's a little skittish, so you might not get close enough to pet him, but you can try. He needs to socialize with humans."

Eva scrambled over the fence.

"Sophia, you keep her safe in there," Mom said.

The colt was in the middle of the pen, his ears alert. He watched as we got closer but didn't seem afraid. His little tail twitched and he pawed at the ground.

"Remember, Eva, don't run. He'll think you're playing and chase you," I said.

She didn't respond, so I looked back to see if she had heard me. She was sprinting back to the fence. *Oh great.*

My eyes were instantly back on the colt. He was jumping in circles. It was my only chance to get a head start, and I took it. "I told you not to run!" I shouted as I got closer to the gate.

"Hurry, Sophia, he's right behind you," Mom said, laughing so hard she was crying.

I wanted to scream at her to stop, to see how serious this was, but I was pumping my arms and legs as fast as I could and couldn't spare the breath.

Eva reached the gate just before me and started to climb. I pushed her up and over before climbing up myself. At the top, I leaped off the gate, falling to the ground just as the colt reached the fence, stopping short and kicking dirt all over me.

"Are you all right?" asked Melissa.

Mom and Eva were laughing.

"I'm fine," I said shortly, trying to catch my breath.

"Why did you run, Eva? We could have gotten hurt," I snapped at her. Mom finally quit laughing.

"I got scared," said Eva.

Standing, I patted the dust off the best I could. Melissa took us to her trailer home for a drink of water, and when Hank returned, he let us go for a short ride on the horses.

"Can I ride Beauty?" I asked.

"Not today, since I just exercised her. How about another time?" said Hank. "I'll take you up to see the caves."

"That would be cool, thanks!"

"Well, I think we've had enough excitement for the day," Mom said. "Let's go home and get cleaned up."

Mom and Eva kept replaying the event with the colt and laughing about it all the way home, so I ran ahead of them, beating them to the cabin.

"How was your—" Edgar stopped mid-sentence after seeing me covered in dirt. "Why are you all dirty?"

I told him about the colt and Eva running. Edgar laughed.

"It's not funny. One of us could have been killed. I bet you wouldn't be laughing if we'd had to go to the hospital," I said.

"But you weren't hurt, Soph. You did good."

"That's just dandy," I said, grabbing a change of clothes and heading to the bathroom to shower. Taking my time, I showered, brushed my hair and teeth, and only came out when Eva pounded on the door, saying she needed to go to the bathroom.

The smell of cooking meat filled the air and my mouth watered.

"What is this?" I asked, entering the kitchen to see a bowl of soup with little balls of rice and meat.

"Venison rice soup," said Edgar.

"What is venison?"

"Deer meat."

I took a bite. There was no seasoning in it, whatsoever. *Yuck.* I stabbed at the meat with my fork. It was tougher than beef, with a tangy flavor. Not too bad, but not the best thing I'd ever eaten. I choked down the unflavored soup. Rice was going on my list of things I would never eat again.

Chapter 31

"I know a dance to this song. Want to see it? I can teach it to you," Melissa said.

We'd gone to her house every day for the past two weeks. Partly for the horses, but also because she had a TV, and when we were bored we watched movies. Today, Melissa had the radio on when we got there. Since the other group believed music had secret messages in it that brainwashed people, we hadn't heard music in a very long time. Eva and I both begged her to keep the radio on for a while.

"I want to learn the dance," Eva said.

I shook my head. "No thanks. I'll watch, but I don't care about dancing."

There was no purpose to it. I would rather learn how to build something, hunt, or go shoot my gun. Those were useful skills to have. Dancing wasn't.

"Please learn it with me, Sophia, so I can practice at home?" begged Eva.

"I have it on cassette tape, so we can practice a couple times," Melissa said.

Eva folded her hands under her chin and knelt in front of me. "Please learn it with me?"

"Fine, I'll write the dance moves down and help you practice, but I don't want to dance," I said.

Melissa disappeared into her room and came back with the tape and a portable player. "Okay, this song is called 'Dancing Under the Stars.' You start like this, with your feet spread apart a little, and your hands on your hips."

Eva got up and copied her. I wrote the instruction down and waited for the next move. They kept at it for half the day and probably would have continued, but I told them I was bored and asked if we could go ride horses.

"It would be a good idea to rest our muscles for a while," Melissa said. "We can practice more if we have energy after our ride."

As promised, Hank let me ride Beauty. She was a great horse, gentle and smart. It seemed like she knew which direction I wanted to go a second before I told her. Like she was reading my mind or something.

The old ship was in front of us. "Hey, can we explore the ship, or is it off-limits?" I asked as we rode by.

"We can go in it as long as we're careful. There are lots of lizards, bugs, and rats, and we've put a lot of traps in there to catch them," Hank said.

"We can do that tomorrow," I said, noticing the sun was getting low.

"Sure," said Melissa.

We rode back to the barn, unsaddled the horses and put them in the corral. By the time we finished, Mom was there to pick us up.

"See you tomorrow. I'll practice the dance so we can be better," Eva said.

"*After* we explore the ship," I corrected. "You guys spent most of today working on that dumb dance, and Melissa promised we could go explore the ship tomorrow."

"The ship is what's dumb, not our dance. I bet Melissa doesn't even want to go to that stupid ship, so it's two against one," said Eva, sticking her tongue out at me.

I rolled my eyes and walked ahead of her.

That evening, Edgar got home later than usual, and when he came into the cabin he had a playful grin on his face. "Girls, I have a present for you."

"What is it?" asked Eva.

"Go outside and see."

We raced out and found a bike leaning against the cabin.

"Cool!" shouted Eva.

"That's for you two to share so you don't have to walk everywhere. It will help get you around the compound faster," said Edgar, smiling.

"Thanks," I said. "We can ride the bike to Melissa's tomorrow. Where should we keep it? Does it have a bike lock?"

"No bike lock. The great thing about living on this compound is that everyone knows what everyone else owns. So you don't have to worry about it being stolen," said Edgar.

"Hurry, Eva," I yelled, sitting on the bike the following morning.

"I have to grab the dance instructions. I'm almost ready," she shouted back from inside the cabin. "Okay, got them," she said, running out and climbing on the back of the bike. It took us much less time to get to Melissa's house on the bike, even with the hill we had to climb.

"I brought the dance instructions," Eva shouted, waving the paper around when Melissa came outside.

"Great, I can't wait to practice," she said, to my dismay.

"We're going to see the ship first though, right?" I said pleadingly.

"Can we go later? It's still kind of cold," said Melissa, who shivered and rubbed her arms as she spoke.

"Oh my gosh, it's the end of March, there isn't any snow and it's not that cold."

Melissa and Eva just stared at me.

"I'll just go by myself," I said.

"Okay, whatever, we'll be here," Melissa replied.

I left the bike at the trailer and walked the short distance to the ship, walking around the outside of it first, looking at the details. The paint on the bottom of the boat had a green tint to it, like it had been in water at one point. There was a big hole in one side. The door turned into a bridge that would let down at a dock. Most of it was buried under dirt, but I could still see some wood peeking through.

I walked aboard and investigated the whole thing, walking slowly and checking each step to avoid any big rat traps. The main deck had a tall mast, broken in half. The top part was lying across the deck. The ship's wheel was chipped, and splintered wood stuck out of it in some places.

It would be fun to play pirates if Eva and Melissa were here. I walked around some more, and Hank was right, there were traps everywhere. One of them had a big rat in it, but the others were empty. It was clear there wasn't anything interesting left to find on this ship. Other people had probably found all the treasure, but I wasn't about to go back to the trailer and watch Melissa and Eva dance on repeat all day.

I decided to check out the red barn some more. Maybe I could see Beauty and pet the other horses. I wandered in, letting my eyes adjust to the dim light. Beauty was in a stall nearby, and I walked up to her.

"Hey, Sophia, how are you doing this fine morning?" asked Hank, who walked up beside me just then and scratched Beauty's nose.

"Good, I decided to come out here because Eva and Melissa are dancing and I don't want to watch them do that all day."

"I was just about to take one of the horses out for some exercise. Would you like to join me? We can go check out those caves I mentioned to you a while back. You can ride Beauty."

A horseback ride and caves sounded great, but going alone with Hank? "I don't think my Mom would be okay with that," I said.

"We'll only be gone an hour, plus there are guys patrolling the border of the compound keeping us safe. You're one of us now, so you can go anywhere on the property you want. The caves I want to take you to haven't been touched by human hands in hundreds of years. There are lots of old things to look at up there."

I hesitated for a moment. Something told me not to go, but I wanted to see the caves so badly. "Okay, let me tell Eva where I'm going."

I took off running toward the trailer. "Eva, Hank wants to take us on a horseback ride to some cool caves, want to go?"

They were mid-routine, but stopped when I entered.

"I've been to those caves before. There's just a bunch of old junk lying around. I'd rather stay here," Melissa said.

"I'd rather stay, too," Eva said.

"Please, Eva, I wrote down all the dance moves for you, even though I don't care about dancing," I said.

She shook her head. "We've almost got the dance down perfectly; we have to keep practicing."

"Fine." I walked back to the barn. Hank seemed nice. He was old and not very strong. Besides, Beauty and I had a connection. She would keep me safe if Hank tried to hurt me.

"Okay, I'm ready."

Hank already had Beauty and another horse saddled.

"Who is this?" I asked.

"This is Midnight. He's a little older than Beauty," Hank said.

"I held out my hand for him to sniff it. "Hi, Midnight. We have a dog back home named Midnight."

He turned his head away, and Beauty nuzzled my shoulder. She seemed happy to see me. The feeling was mutual.

"Ready to go?" asked Hank.

"Yep," I said, climbing onto Beauty's back.

We headed toward the mountain behind the corral. Neither of us spoke much but took in the surroundings as we rode. This place was beautiful. Once we got around the corral we were headed into thick pine trees. This was the only other place I'd seen trees on the ranch since we'd been there.

We followed a well-maintained trail up the mountain, and after a while the pine trees thinned out. We went around several curves, but finally I could see the caves up ahead. The entrances looked small, but there were a lot of them.

"Here we are," said Hank. "Just down this hill there is a wooden post we can tie the horses to."

"Can I explore the whole thing?" I asked.

"Yeah, just don't touch anything. It will be worth a lot of money someday, if it isn't already."

We got to the post, climbed off our horses and tied them up. I jogged to one of the caves and walked in, being careful not to step on any of the clay pots scattered on the floor.

The mouth of the cave was wide and let in just enough sunlight so I could inspect all the pictures of deer, people, and tents that covered the wall. One image looked like a person with some kind of headdress on, holding a staff and a shield.

I inspected each clay pot and found several arrowheads lying in a corner. If only I could have one.

Hank watched me from a log over by the horses. When I had explored every inch of the place, I joined him. "I'm ready to go now," I said.

"Let's not leave quite yet," said Hank. "Come over here and sit next to me. I want to talk to you for a minute."

"Is everything okay? I didn't touch anything," I said.

"Yes, everything is fine. I know you obeyed me. You're a good girl." He patted the spot next to him. I sat, but angled myself away from him in case I needed to get up and run.

He wrapped his arm around my waist and stuck one finger barely inside my pants, near my hip.

"My wife and I have been having problems lately. She doesn't understand my point of view. Things have been getting really bad around here, and no one will listen to what I have to say about it. This is my land, after all. Plus, my wife has denied me for a while now," Hank said. He stared off into the distance and seemed to forget I was there for a moment.

I knew what it felt like to not be listened to. Hank seemed sad and lonely, and I wanted to be a good friend to him, but I didn't understand what he meant about his wife. If there were problems on the compound, that probably meant we would have to leave soon.

Hank rested his other hand on my knee. "Have you heard about the birds and the bees?"

What was he talking about? Was there something wrong with the birds and the bees, too? The way he was talking made me nervous.

"It doesn't hurt, you know. A little at first, but it goes in like a bullet."

Did he need a doctor? What on earth was he talking about?

"Men have certain needs that only a woman can provide. When a man is denied those needs, he can get depressed and lonely." His hand moved up my thigh.

My heart beat faster.

"You're a good, sweet girl. You could help me out, be my special friend, right?" asked Hank, leaning over and putting his nose in my hair.

I remembered how my stepbrother, Isaac's ex-wife's son, had asked me to be his special friend when I was five, and touched my private places. I'd told Mom while she was doing my hair the next morning and she hit me over the head with the brush, said that kind of stuff was serious, and told me not to make up stories like that. Now I understood what Hank wanted. How was I going to get out of this mess?

Hank squeezed me closer to him with the arm that was around my waist. His other hand dug into my stomach as he tried to get his fingers into my pants. "The patrol will come by here soon, so I'll be quick," whispered Hank.

I grabbed his hands and stood up quickly, shoving his arms away from me as I moved away from him. "I want to go home now. My mom is probably looking for me," I said, running over to the horses, who, thankfully, were not very far away. I untied Beauty as quickly as I could and mounted her without trouble.

Hank grabbed my leg, "If you tell anyone about this, I'll kill you."

I stared down at him, the once-kind eyes now hard, his grip tight on my leg.

"I won't tell anyone, I promise."

I rode hard all the way back to the barn. Once there, I jumped off Beauty and ran home before Hank was off his horse. I didn't expect anyone to be there because it was still early in the day, but Mom and Eva were both there.

"Where have you been?" Mom asked.

I told her everything. When I finished my story, Mom paced the floor, not saying anything. I watched her face. Did she believe me? Would she do something about it? Would we have to leave again?

Finally she stopped in front of me. "Stay here with your sister, and don't let anyone in the cabin."

Mom left, slamming the door behind her.

"I told Mom you went for a horseback ride with Hank but couldn't remember where you said you were going," said Eva.

"It's okay." I was relieved Eva was here and not at Melissa's. Would Hank have tried anything with Eva if he'd found her by herself? I shuddered at the thought and wondered what would happen when Mom came back.

Chapter 32

"Do you want to see if we can go find more diamond dinosaur feet?" Eva asked, when we'd been waiting for Mom's return for almost an hour.

"Sure," I said, deciding it would be better than sitting around with nothing to do except worry.

We went outside, and I closed the door behind me. "Oh, shoot."

"What?" asked Eva.

"I forgot to pull the leather string through the door. We'll have to climb through the bathroom window when we go back inside."

Eva shrugged. It wasn't the first time. "Okay."

We dug for over an hour before Mom returned, and we heard her before we saw her.

"Sophia, let me in this minute." I heard her pound on the cabin door and jumped up and ran to her.

"I'm right here," I said.

"Is anyone inside?"

"No."

Eva ran up and stood beside me as I answered.

"So you forgot to pull the leather string through? How are we supposed to get back into the cabin?" Her face was turning red.

"I know a way, Mom, I'm sorry." I ran around the side of the cabin, dug the Swiss army knife out of my pocket, pulled out the screwdriver and unscrewed the screen. After taking it off the window, I slid the pane up, crawled through and ran to the door. As I reached for the handle I paused. Mom was really upset. What would she do?

I swung the door open, putting it between me and Mom, but that didn't stop her. She reached around the door, grabbed my hair, and threw me to the ground. I looked up at her, lifting my arms as I did to ward off any more attack. Her eyes were black. She kicked me, and I curled into a ball as her foot made contact with my body a second time. I rolled over, trying to protect myself the best I could from her continued kicking.

Help me, someone please help me.

A calmness came over me, or maybe I was just numb, but fear had disappeared. It was replaced with anger. After another blow to my back, I scrambled to my feet and faced her. Mom started forward, her fists clenched.

"Stop!" I yelled, staring her in the eyes. "You will not touch me ever again, do you hear me?"

Mom froze, staring at me. I felt like I was towering over her. I also felt older and stronger. I kept staring at her until her body relaxed and tears filled her eyes. She blinked several times, then looked away.

"I'm so sorry, baby. I have no idea what came over me. Will you forgive me?"

I didn't respond. Instead, I walked around her, out the open door, and headed to the lake to be alone. Eva had returned to the dirt pile. I had no idea what she'd seen or heard, but she didn't see me leave. I found a grassy spot near the water and sat down. My whole body felt shaky and I had a hard time catching my breath, but I didn't feel afraid.

Eventually my body stopped shaking and my breathing returned to normal. Something in me felt different. Stronger. I am not sure what happened to make her treat me like that, but I did not care. I would get through this, and no one would hurt me ever again. Even if I had to deal with these people until I was as adult, I would be okay.

When I finally went back to the house, Mom tried to give me a hug, but I wouldn't let her touch me. She kept apologizing, and I'm sure she meant it, but I ignored her. I would not trust her to protect us anymore.

"Girls, we need to make a trip to the big house before you run off to play today," said Mom. "Since Edgar and I aren't quite ready, why don't you two head up on your bike and we'll meet you there."

Two days had passed since the incident with Hank, and Mom had told me nothing about what she'd done or said in response. I refused to go back to Melissa's house. Eva wasn't too happy about it, and I had finally agreed to take her up there this morning so she could ask Melissa to come play with us at the cabin, just to stop her from complaining. But now we'd have to wait until we were done at the big white house, which was fine with me. Unless Melissa was there, and then we wouldn't have to go at all.

We climbed onto the bike, and I cringed when Eva touched my back. It was still sore from the events from two days before. We got about halfway before Mom and Edgar passed us in the truck. When we reached the house, they were out front, talking with Kevin. So we weren't here for a meeting? Were we in trouble?

"Sophia, Edgar tells me you're good with a gun," said Kevin.

"I'm okay," I said, trying not to sound proud of myself.

"Hold this one, see if it's too heavy for you." He handed me a small, camouflaged rifle with a red scope on top.

I tested the weight by lifting it up and down in my hands. "It's heavy, but I can lift it."

"Look through the scope. Can you see our nation's flag?"

I aimed the gun toward the flag that flew on top of the house and looked through the scope again. "I can see it."

"Great, tell me what it says on the flag."

The wind made it hard to read the words, but after a few minutes, I saw what it said. "United we stand."

Kevin stretched his arm out, and I handed him back the gun. He took a full magazine out of this pocket and put it in the gun.

"Excellent. If you see someone you don't recognize, I want you to shoot them," said Kevin, handing the now loaded rifle back to me. "Just aim through the scope and pull the trigger."

"You can't be serious," said Mom, grabbing the firearm from my hand.

"Unfortunately, Grace, I am."

"But she's only ten."

"Edgar told us they trained her to handle guns at the militia house you stayed in. So well, in fact, she is a better shot than most of us. We don't want to kill anyone, but we've experienced enough thieves and government agents on our land that we've developed a shoot-now, ask-questions-later approach. The more people we have armed, the better," Kevin said.

Mom pointed the rifle toward the front gate of the compound and glanced through the scope. "You mean like the FBI who are rolling up with their tanks right now?

We all looked in the direction she pointed. Several armored vehicles with the letters FBI on the sides made their way along the fence line before coming to a stop. I turned to Mom and noted that she was holding the gun sideways with her finger curled around the trigger of a loaded weapon pointed at the FBI.

And I'm the one who's not allowed to use a gun.

"Yes, exactly like that. Quickly, follow me to the house," said Kevin.

As we made our way inside, people starting running toward us from all over. They must have had some way to communicate with each other fast, because in a few minutes everyone living in Freedom Township was in the big meeting room.

"All right, guys and gals, listen up," Kevin shouted over the noise. "This is the day we've planned for; no one is allowed to leave the ranch right now, as it poses a risk and could jeopardize this whole operation. It's time to protect our land, so for your safety and ours, please don't set foot off the property.

"As for food and water, we have enough to feed an army for several years. The ten silos are full of wheat and corn, and the springs give us plenty to drink. Plus, we have a few skilled hunters in our ranks.

"Moving on, those parasites need to see the children. They know we won't go down without a fight, and they have a lot more firepower than we do with those tanks. The FBI won't put the kids in harm's way, which means they'll keep their distance and not force their way in."

"Mommy, what are they talking about?" whispered Eva.

I knew what they were talking about. It was the bus all over again. They were going to make me, Eva, and Melissa walk out there so the FBI could see us. At least Stewart wasn't here. He would probably tell us we were sinful for some weird reason, then tie us to a pole.

"Baby, we need you and Sophia to play a game. You're both shields, and nothing can hurt you."

Eva leaped to her feet. "Not even bullets?"

Mom winced, and I cringed.

"Correct, not even bullets. It's up to you and your sister to keep everyone here safe from the bad government agents. It's a very important job. Right, Sophia?"

I stared at her, not at all surprised she would put us in danger again because of what some crazy nut jobs told her to do. "Right, Mom, no one will hurt us because we're shields," I said sarcastically. I folded my arms and slumped back in the chair.

Mom wrapped her arm around me, pulled me close to her and whispered, "You'll be safe, and we will get out. I promise."

Yeah, right.

"Sophia, you and Eva take the bicycle and ride around while we finish here, but don't get too close to the fence," Edgar said.

I knew it was best to do what we were told. The people at the bar hadn't noticed or cared that a kid was in the doorway of the bus they were shooting at, but it was dark and they were probably drunk. It was daylight now, and these people were trained. Kevin was probably right; they would see us riding around and wouldn't shoot.

Eva jumped, twirled, and danced her way outside, oblivious to the danger we were in.

"Eva, get on the bike," I snapped.

She obeyed, and I started to pedal.

We got close enough to the fence to see a lot of police and people wearing dark blue jackets with yellow FBI letters on the back. Some of them held up binoculars to watch us. Eva waved at them. Many of them motioned for us to come over, but we kept our distance.

One held up a bullhorn and shouted, "Girls, it's not safe for you there. Trust us, we can protect you."

We rode our bike, ignoring their shouts and gestures. I'd always been taught the police and FBI were good and would help us, but for the past eight months, everyone had kept telling us not to trust them. I didn't know what to believe anymore, but I wasn't going to go over there if Mom wasn't with us. They'd seen us, and our job as human shields was finished for the day. I pedaled as fast as I could back to the house.

"Great job," Edgar said as we got off the bike.

Mom stood next to him, and a group of people were gathered around them, including Brooke and Hank.

"Get off, Eva, we're going to put the bike in the back of the truck," I said, exhausted and ready to go home to the cabin.

"You girls were brave today," Brooke said.

"Where is Melissa?" Eva asked Brooke.

"She left this morning with Daniel, to get some supplies. They won't come back here. He'll take care of her until this is all over," she said.

"All right, girls, let's head home, we have a lot to discuss," Edgar said.

Back at the cabin, we all gathered in the living room.

"What's the plan, dear?" Mom asked.

"The FBI are going to try to negotiate something to get us all off this land so they can come in. Because of the kids, we are the bargaining chip. Grace, this is a big deal. I suspect both the FBI and the people living here are expecting a huge fight, and the only question is, are we prepared to stick it out and see what happens, do we want to make a deal with the FBI, or do we want to try and sneak off somehow through the forest?"

"Well, we don't have much of a choice, do we?" Mom said. "It's too much of a risk taking two children through the woods. We don't know if the FBI have us totally surrounded, but we have to assume they're watching every inch of the border. I would rather stay and negotiate something that will work out for everyone involved, don't you think so?"

"What do you girls think? Should we stay and fight and see what happens?" Edgar asked.

Eva and I looked at each other, then back to Edgar and Mom.

"What is going to happen?" I asked.

"Well, the worst case is, we stick it out until the FBI decides to force their way in. In which case, we'd hole up here and try not to get shot."

I guess he saw the fear on our faces, because he quickly added, "We'd be okay. The cabin is bulletproof."

I rolled my eyes, but before we could ask any more questions, there was a knock at the door. Edgar got up and answered it.

A voice I didn't recognize asked, "So, what is your plan?"

"We're staying," said Edgar.

"Glad to hear. We'll regroup tomorrow. In the meantime, we have a few people stationed at your door. There are several guns with ammo in a hidden compartment under the rug in the kitchen, should you need it."

I got up and rolled up the rug. There was a hole in the floor that looked like a handle. Of all the places I'd investigated, I'd never once thought to look under the rugs.

"Thank you sir," said Edgar, and he closed the door.

Chapter 33

A little over a week had passed since the FBI had surrounded the compound. They'd turned off the water supply, but no one was very concerned about that, because they'd stored enough bottled water to last for years, and we could bathe in the lake. I wasn't worried about them shooting at us anymore. Eva and I rode the bike around every day to see what they were up to. Mostly they spoke into walkie-talkies, looked through binoculars and sat around next to the armored vehicles on camping chairs. I think they gave up trying to convince us to go to them, because they stopped shouting at us.

Men patrolled our side of the fence, and if we got too close, they yelled at us to get back. It felt pretty safe, and we soon knew how close we could get without getting yelled at. The most exciting thing that happened was the blue canopy the FBI put up near the entrance. It was early April, and the days were getting warmer.

"They must be hot," said Eva.

"Yeah, we should tell Mom and Edgar," I said.

We rode back to the cabin and found Brooke inside, talking to Mom.

"Sophia, I'm so glad I got to see you before I left. Here is the lavender and mint soap you made. I keep forgetting to give it to your mom, so I decided I'd just bring it to you instead." Brooke held the soap bar out to me.

I'd completely forgotten about it. I grinned and took it from her hand, putting it up to my nose.

"I love that combination you picked; I think it's my favorite now," she said.

"Thank you, I can't wait to use it." I slipped it into my suitcase so no one else would use it.

After Brooke left, we told Mom about the canopy, and she started pacing back and forth.

"Don't worry, girls, we're safe here."

I shook my head. She wasn't very convincing. "What's wrong?" I asked.

"Nothing, baby, it just means I need to talk to them soon and your aunt Audrey mailed me a letter, so I know she'll be here soon as well." Mom stopped pacing and sat on the couch.

"Can I read it?" I asked.

"No, baby, you don't need to concern yourself with adult matters."

"Mom, are the FBI bad?" asked Eva. But before Mom could even think about answering, she went on, "What are they doing here? Why are they surrounding us?"

Eva had been asking me these questions, but I couldn't answer them. I had tried to tell her not to bug Mom with them, but I guess she couldn't keep it in any longer.

"Not all of them are bad," said Mom. "I'm not completely sure why they're here or why they surrounded us, but I promise they won't hurt you, me, or Sophia. There are plenty of armed men all around us, Eva, so you really don't need to worry. I promise, we're safe here."

"Okay, Mommy, if you say so."

A lump formed in my throat and I tried to swallow it, but it was useless. I let out a sob. "Safe? We're safe here?" I yelled. "What were you thinking? Why are we here? Why can't we go back home? I miss Sapphira—where is she? I want to know where she is, right now!"

Eva stared at me, eyes wide. Mom got up, walked over to me and wrapped me in her arms. "It's okay, baby. Sapphira is safe. She's probably at home with our family right now. I knew it was only a matter of time before you broke down. You haven't been yourself for quite some time now." Mom kissed my forehead. "Edgar has gone to find a way for us to leave. This isn't our battle, and we don't need to be in the middle of it."

I covered my face with my hands and sobbed. After a few minutes, I felt calmer and used my shirt to wipe the tears from my face.

"Better?" Mom asked.

I didn't respond. I felt empty inside.

"You cry like a skeleton," said Eva.

"Shut up, that doesn't even make sense," I said.

Mom and Eva both laughed.

"Am I the only one who understands how serious this situation is?" I asked, before storming outside and slamming the door behind me.

Mom just told Eva a bunch of stories to make her believe we were safe. Was Edgar really looking for a way out, or was that another story? I walked over to the dirt pile and dug my fingers into the soil, wishing we were back home doing all the normal things we used to do. The camping, fishing, horseback riding, and learning how to shoot had been fun, but I was ready to go home.

I thought about the letter Aunty wrote to Mom. Why wouldn't she let me read it? There had to be clues in it as to what was going on and what would happen next.

"Always remember who you are. You have a light in you. Don't let it go out. Don't let them take it from you." Sapphira's words to me the day after the bus shooting came back to me. I hadn't understood what she meant—still didn't, really—but I think I was starting to figure it out.

April came and went, and May was well on its way and the FBI still surrounded the place, with little change in routine except they'd cut off the power to the compound. Little did they know we had plenty of generators, and fuel to run them. Eva and I still rode the bike around, but we didn't pay much attention to what was happening outside the compound anymore. It had become normal to see them staring at us with their binoculars.

One morning, Eva and I were out riding when Edgar and Mom pulled up beside us in the truck. "Girls, get in," Mom said.

Eva hopped off, and I tossed the bike in back before climbing in.

"Where are we going?" I asked.

"Remember the blue canopy?"

"Yes."

"We're going there to negotiate us leaving the ranch."

"Do you think we'll get to leave today?" I asked.

"Possibly, but we need you two to do exactly what we say."

"Yeah, your mom is going to talk to them, which means you and Eva need to stay back with me," Edgar said. "We don't want them trying to lure you away from us. Got it?"

"Got it," Eva and I answered in unison.

"We're here. Now, you two stay right with Edgar," Mom said. "When he stops, you stop. No matter what happens, you stay with him, okay?"

We both nodded, and she kissed each of us on the head before walking the few yards to the canopy. Once there, she hugged someone. I wasn't sure who the person was for a moment, but when they stopped hugging I could see her face more clearly. It was Aunt Audrey! She looked our way and waved, and I waved back.

"Look, Eva, it's Aunt Audrey." I started walking toward her, wanting to hug her as well, but Edgar put his hand on my shoulder and stopped me.

"That's far enough for now, Sophia. Let's wait and see what happens."

"What do you think they're talking about?" Eva asked.

"Not sure, let's see if I can read their lips," I said, focusing on the agent's mouth. "Nope, I can't tell."

One of the agents handed Mom some papers. She spent several minutes reading through them, then handed them back. She didn't look happy. After they argued back and forth for a while, one of the agents stooped over the table, wrote something down, then handed the documents back to Mom.

This process was repeated several times over the course of thirty minutes or so, before Mom threw the papers in their faces and walked back toward us.

"Let's go," she said, storming past us.

We scrambled into the truck. Everyone was silent until we reached the cabin.

"What happened, Grace?" Edgar asked.

"They want us to go back to Utah, give Audrey temporary custody of the girls, and throw us both in jail," said Mom, struggling to keep back her tears.

"What did Audrey say?" asked Edgar.

"She wants to take the girls. She wants me to go to jail and then she wants me to pay her child support once I get out."

"That's no good. What else did they say?"

"They're going to redo the documents and we'll talk again tomorrow. Same place, same time."

Chapter 34

Over the next two weeks, Mom met with them four more times. Each time turned out the same. Mom came back frustrated and close to tears. The FBI hadn't really changed the agreement, just the way they worded it.

During this time, Daniel's dad took us on helicopter rides. We didn't leave the ranch, and pretty much just went up and down. The blue helicopter was small and had a big windshield. It wasn't very loud when it started, either. Daniel called it a "Blue Stealth-O-Copter." When he wasn't using the helicopter, the pad it was parked on was covered with tons of old tires.

After the fifth meeting, Mom returned to us smiling.

"We're getting close to a deal. We'll get to go home soon."

Her words echoed in my head. Home. Was it really possible?

We returned to the canopy the second week of June. This meeting lasted longer than the other ones, and there was a buzz of activity around the tent. Something was about to happen, and I couldn't tear my eyes away.

Finally, Mom rushed over to us. "Girls, let's go get our things. We're going home."

"Really?" asked Eva.

"Really, really. Where is Edgar?"

"He is over there talking to the agents." Eva pointed.

"Our real home, or a new place?" I asked.

"Home to Salt Lake. Your Aunt Audrey is waiting to take us to the airport," said Mom.

We drove back to the cabin for the last time, packed our things as quickly as we could, and loaded them into the car. Back at the canopy, federal agents greeted us with smiles.

"Hello, I'm Agent Green, and this is Agent Marks."

Agent Green was tall and husky, with dark brown hair and green eyes. He appeared to be around Edgar's age. Agent Marks was younger, wore a cowboy hat, and had red hair poking out from behind his ears. His eyes were blue, and he had a mustache that matched his red hair.

"You must be Sophia." Agent Green stuck his hand out for me to shake. I nodded and shook his hand. "And you must be Eva," he said, turning to my little sister and offering her his hand as well.

"I'm really excited we were able to work things out so you girls can go home. Please follow me to the tent, where we have some cool things for you while we wait for the others to finish arranging your flight back to Utah."

"Thank you, sir," Edgar said.

We all climbed into the car and followed them. I looked behind us and saw another black SUV turn in to follow us from out of nowhere.

"Grace, they're going to take you and the girls to the airport. Not me. I will be arrested, and after a few years I will come find you," said Edgar.

"How do you know that?" I asked.

"Because that was part of the final arrangements to make sure you're all safe," he said.

Mom stared out the front window with a blank expression on her face. "Okay," she said dully.

We pulled up to a giant green tent the size of a house. I grabbed Wooby before climbing out of the car.

Federal Agent Marks asked us to follow him along some wooden boards they'd placed over mud and water holes. Once inside, we saw Aunt Audrey, and she pulled each of us in for a hug. Seeing her was like waking up from a horrible dream.

"I'm so glad you're all safe," she said.

"I'm so happy to see you," I said, choking back tears.

"If you girls follow us," interrupted Agent Marks, "you can pick out some cool souvenirs."

Aunt Audrey came with us, but Mom and Edgar hung back. I hesitated, not wanting to go if Mom didn't come with us. Aunty seemed to understand this and wrapped her arm around my shoulder, leading me forward. "Your mom will join us soon. She is saying her goodbyes to Edgar."

The giant tent had multiple rooms, and all the agents we passed greeted us with waves and smiles. We entered one of the rooms, and it was set up like a fair, with booths lining the walls full of stuff like flashlights, binoculars, different styles of hats and shirts, all with the FBI logo on them. Aunt Audrey would only let us accept a hat and a shirt, and helped us find our sizes.

Two female agents walked up to us while we tried on the shirts. "Hi, there. I'm Federal Agent Rednour, and this is Agent Joy. We'll be with staying with you until you reach Utah. Is there anything we can get you right now, or anything special you'd like to eat or drink on the plane trip home?"

"Where is the bathroom?" I asked.

"Do you see those little green buildings over there?" asked Agent Rednour, pointing to the other side of the giant tent.

"Yes," I said.

"I'll take them," said Aunt Audrey. "Come on, girls."

While Eva and I were using the restroom, I heard Mom ask her where we were.

"They're in there."

"Good, when we get back to Utah I will meet you at your house. You did say you still have an extra house key, right?"

"Yes, I do still have an extra key," Audrey said.

"We just got word that the plane is fueled and ready to go," said a familiar man's voice. I guessed it was either Agent Green or Marks. "We won't handcuff Edgar until you're on your way to the airport. We don't want them traumatized any more than they already are."

Traumatized? What were they talking about? I was happy to be going home. I finished my business, washed my hands, and stepped out. Agents Rednour and Joy had joined Mom, Aunt Audrey, and Eva.

"Everyone ready to go?" asked Agent Joy.

"I believe so," Mom said.

We followed the agents to a black SUV and climbed in. Another SUV, identical to ours, followed behind us, and a cop car drove in front of us with its lights on. The drive took just over an hour, but we finally arrived at the airport. The car drove us right onto the tarmac and stopped in front of a white plane that said "United States Government" on the side in bold, green letters.

"Okay, all aboard the Salt Lake Express," said Agent Joy.

We all climbed out of the SUV and mounted the stairs to the airplane. I'd only ever seen celebrities and presidents get on a plane like this. It was awesome to get such special treatment.

"Follow me. I'll show you to your seats so we can get buckled and ready to go. Your luggage will be put on board by other agents," said Agent Rednour.

We boarded the plane, but it wasn't like any plane I'd ever seen. There were only two seats on each row, and every chair swiveled around. Between each set of four seats was a table that could be folded and laid on the floor so the seats could be transformed into beds. There was also a couch at the back of the plane, and a full-sized bathroom.

We took our seats and Mom helped us buckle in. Once we were all settled, it was only a few minutes before we were in the air. Eva and I both had window seats, and we watched as the cars on the ground got smaller and smaller. Agents Joy and Rednour gave us snacks and drinks and let us watch a movie on a big screen that pulled down out of the ceiling at the front of the plane.

Before we knew it, the pilot announced we were landing.

"Girls, when we get off the plane, you're going to go with your Aunt Audrey, okay?" Mom said. "I'll be right behind you."

When the plane stopped, the door was opened and stairs were rolled to the door. The agents unbuckled us, and Mom hugged us and pushed us toward the door. "Everything is going to be okay. I'll see you soon."

We climbed down the stairs and were led into the airport. I was immediately blinded by flashing lights. People were shouting at us and taking our pictures. Someone shoved a microphone in my face before a police officer pushed them away.

"Mom?" I looked over my shoulder, but there were too many people and I couldn't see her.

Aunt Audrey grabbed my hand and Eva's. "Come on, girls, this way. We're almost out of here."

We were led into a hallway away from the people, and at the end stood my stepmom, Paula, my birth dad, Dennis, and Eva's dad, Isaac.

"What are they doing here?" asked Aunt Audrey.

"There was a last-minute change of plans," said Agent Joy, who walked behind us. "The girls are now in the custody of Dennis and Paula."

"What?" Audrey stopped, dropped our hands and turned to face Agent Joy. "That's not what we agreed on. Does Grace know about this?"

"The agreement we made with you was in the state of Montana. I have documents here, signed by Grace, giving custody to Dennis and Paula once the girls reach Utah. Thank you for helping us bring them home safely," the agent said.

I grabbed Eva's hand and ran toward the others. The closer we got, the bigger their smiles were, and by the time we were done hugging each other, we were all crying.

"We've missed you both so much," said Isaac, hugging us both tightly and kissing our cheeks over and over. "Eva, you're going to stay with Sophia, but I'm going to see you all the time," he promised.

"Where is Mom?" I asked, after the first wave of excitement had passed.

"She'll be here soon," Paula said.

A few minutes later, Mom joined us, followed by two police officers. "Okay, girls, there's been a change of plans. Sophia and Eva, you're going to stay with Paula and Dennis for a while. I have some things I have to take care of. We'll be able to talk on the phone, and I'll write you letters every day. I love you both very much, and I'm so sorry you had to go through all of this."

The three of us hugged each other tightly and cried.

"I'm going to get the car," said Dennis.

"I love you, Mommy. I will be with Daddy, so you don't need to worry," Eva said.

"Don't forget to call and write us," I said, wondering where Mom was going and how long she would be gone.

"Time to go now," said Agent Rednour, who kept looking back over her shoulder. I could tell she was worried about the media and wanted to rush to get us out of there.

"Love you, Mom, see you soon," I said.

I took Paula's hand and Eva took her dad's hand, and we walked outside to the car Dennis had just pulled up in.

"Let's all get some lunch," said Isaac.

Everyone agreed to this plan. As we drove away, I glanced out the back window and saw Mom waving. I started crying again. I was happy to be home, but I knew my life would never be the same.

Chapter 35

"How are you doing?" asked Stacy. "You look pale. That was a lot to share and remember."

I took a sip of water. "I'm good, thanks. It's definitely hard to relive some of the memories, but it feels good to talk about it. I've actually wanted to write a book about it but could never bring myself to do it."

"That's an interesting idea. We have someone in our church who writes books; maybe you could talk to her."

"Oh, that's cool. I'll have to think about it," I said.

"So why did the FBI surround the ranch?" asked Stacy.

"I was told they'd been monitoring the ranch and the militia people for some time because they knew there was illegal activity going on with bank fraud.

"When we got there, it added another layer to the situation because, like I said earlier, Sapphira's uncle had helped my stepdad Isaac by hiring a private investigator to find us. Plus, the police in each of the cities we stayed in were on the lookout for us because of the custody case between my mom and Isaac. So my best guess is all these agencies decided to join forces when they figured out we were on the ranch."

"That is really amazing. Did you ever find out what happened to Melissa? Was she reunited with her mom?"

"I don't know. I never heard."

Stacy sat back in her chair. "Wow, I know you said it was exhausting reliving and telling your story. I believe it, I only had to listen and my emotions have been all over the place. How are you feeling about these sessions? Do you want to continue? Would you like to take some time to think it over?"

"Now that I've shared my story with you, where do we go from here?"

"Well, we've already started the process of biblical counseling, so we'd continue to meet weekly, but start diving deeper. I would also like to take you through a Bible-based healing process. I call it Bible healing boot camp. I think it would help you heal from the trauma you experienced as a child and through your life growing up. My hope is, as we go through this part together you will see how God had his hand on you during that time. Would you be interested?" Stacy asked.

I hesitated for only a moment. The whole God thing still made me nervous, but I decided why not, if it will help me grow, let's do it. I stood up and hugged her. "I would love that, thank you for letting me tell you my story."

"I'm glad you trusted me enough to share it. I'll see you at our session next week."

Every spare minute I had after that meeting was spent reading the Bible. I was so curious and I wanted to know more about God and if he was real. So much of what I read didn't make sense to me, but I couldn't stop reading. I was drawn to the Bible like a magnet.

I called Stacy constantly and asked her to explain what I was reading. We would talk for hours on the phone, she was so patient and didn't try to pressure me to join some religion.

I found myself only wanting to listen to a Christian radio station because I liked how I felt afterwards. I faithfully listened to Pastor Kayzik's messages on the radio every Wednesday when I had to make deliveries for work. Everything this pastor said sounded like he was saying it just for me.

Two days later, after work, I called Stacy in tears. "What just happened to me?"

"What are you talking about? Are you okay?" she asked.

"I can barely see through my tears and the rain," I said as I drove home from work.

"Maybe you should pull over and tell me what's going on."

"I'm on the freeway and can't pull over right now. I was listening to the radio, and this guy was talking about how to give your heart to God. I've been questioning everything, and I want to know the truth. I had to know if God was real, so I figured, what could go wrong?

My life feels dead, I haven't been happy, and I wanted to know if there was more to my existence, so I just said 'okay' in response to what the guy on the radio was saying, then shut it off.

I told God I couldn't live like this anymore, and I told Him I needed to know if he was real. I asked Him to forgive me of my sins and help me, because I'm miserable. And now I can't stop crying."

"Well, sweetie, you've just accepted the salvation God has for you. Jesus died on the cross for our sins so we could be saved. You just received that salvation."

Postscript

The FBI standoff lasted a total of 81 days. Not too long after Sophia and her family left Freedom Township, those who remained on the ranch surrendered peacefully.

Kevin was sent to jail on multiple charges including bank fraud, mail fraud, and false claims to the IRS. He died in jail of natural causes at the age of 73. The fate of all the other people on the ranch after they surrendered is unknown.

Edgar was sentenced to five years in jail for illegally buying and selling guns. When he was released, he attempted to reconnect with Grace on several occasions and even bought Sophia her first car when she turned 16, but he was unsuccessful in his attempts to win Grace back.

Grace was sent to jail for five years for leaving the state of Utah during a custody case for Eva and Sophia and for claiming another man as Sophia's father.

Sapphira gave birth to a little girl on the same day Sophia and her family left the compound. She was reconnected with her family soon after Sophia and Eva returned to Utah, and all three sisters have a good relationship today.

Sophia never heard from, or about, Jamie and Chris again, but still has fond memories of her time at their house and still wishes she could find a way to connect with them again.

Stewart was convicted of conspiracy to commit rape and conspiracy to commit sexual abuse of a child, as well as two second-degree felonies unrelated to this story. He remains in prison to this day. It is unknown what happened to the other members of the cult after they were separated.

A Note to Readers

Dear Reader,

I came from a life of dysfunction. Between the time I was four and my teens, I had experiences of being sexually molested and raped. I moved out on my own at the age of seventeen and never looked back. By twenty-two I was dating both men and women. Eventually, I stopped dating men altogether because it felt safer.

Contacting "Stacy" scared me. It was easier to run from my past, pretend it hadn't happened. But I knew I was broken, I knew I needed help, and I was at the end of myself, with nowhere else to turn. Through my conversations with Stacy I chose to give my life to Jesus, and that one decision has forever changed my life for the better.

Stacy helped a lot with the healing process. I even lived with Andy and Stacy for a time, and they helped me get back on my feet in more ways than one. Stacy walked me through a healing process that helped me to forgive myself and those involved in the horrible circumstances of my past. I also came to realize that the lifestyle I'd chosen to live was the result of the childhood trauma I'd endured.

This has allowed me to get to a place where the events in this book are now a part of my story, but they no longer affect my everyday life. It took time for me to be able to recognize the connection. But learning that God forgives me, no matter what, has helped me get to a place where I can forgive others. I don't think I would have been able to get to this place if I didn't have God in my life, and I would still be stuck in anger.

Following Christ is a journey of relationship, not of judgment or oppression. I was taught at a young age not to question what those in religious authority told me to believe, but during the healing process I learned to question what people said and compare what they said to what the Bible says. It was very freeing to learn this and helped me grow in many ways, including how to trust others more.

I had a hard time getting close to people for a long time because I was certain I would be hurt by them. As I went through the healing process, I came to realize this is something I had an issue with, and I began to recognize how my past had affected my relationships. There was a difficult period during the healing process when I wasn't sure if my emotions were being triggered by my past, or if I was genuinely feeling emotions about present circumstances, and I'm so grateful for the small circle of people who were able to help me through that difficult time.

I learned, through spending time getting to know the character of God, that a father is loving, merciful, and kind. A father wants the best for you and wants a relationship with you. In learning about God as a Father, I realized my stepfather, Eva's dad, had always been those things for me. He was and continues to be a positive influence in my life that I cherish more every day.

Because of my decision to accept Christ into my life, I've lost friends who I had thought of as family, because they assumed I would judge them and the lifestyle I left. Although I've found freedom from the pain of my past, I've also found a deeper understanding of love. God's love is so much more powerful than the love any human can offer. It doesn't judge, but embraces and welcomes, and I continue to pray for restored relationships.

I know there is so much more I can learn and grow from in all this, and I welcome it. Life is hard, and it is what you make of it, but I can promise you that whatever wrong has happened to you in your life, God can use it for good. Writing this book was a huge part of the healing process for me, as it brought up some very painful memories that I had to relive and process through as I put it into writing.

I would like to encourage you. Life will send you curve balls, but no matter where you are in your life's journey, keep pushing through—because you are never alone. God can and will change your life if you let Him. God loves you no matter what you've done, and He is eager for you to get to know Him. There is nothing He can't do.

I also want to tell you that salvation and grace are free. You don't have to work for it. You don't have to try to look better than the next person, because it's not about what you do or whether you have done enough to get into heaven. It is simply accepting Jesus into your heart, asking Him to forgive you for your sins, and letting Him guide you in your next steps.

It is God, after all, who created the heavens and the earth and YOU. So I encourage you to take the next step and see for yourself, if you haven't already. Thank you for joining us on the journey. I pray God reveals His love to you where you are.

Many Blessings,
Courtnie